LIVE LIKE
You're
BLESSED

DR. SUZAN JOHNSON COOK

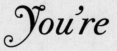

LIVE LIKE
You're
BLESSED

Simple Steps for Making

Balance, Love,

Energy, Spirit,

Success, Encouragement,

and Devotion

Part of Your Life

Doubleday
New York London Toronto Sydney Auckland

PUBLISHED BY DOUBLEDAY
a division of Random House, Inc.

DOUBLEDAY and the portrayal of an anchor with a dolphin
are registered trademarks of Random House, Inc.

Book design by Michael Collica

Cataloging-in-Publication Data is on file with the Library of Congress

ISBN-13: 978-0-385-51719-5
ISBN-10: 0-385-51719-X

In loving memory of my parents, Dorothy C. and
Wilbert T. Johnson, who lived the blessed life

CONTENTS

Contents

ACKNOWLEDGMENTS

In Luke's Gospel, the angel tells Mary, "Rejoice, highly favored one; . . . *blessed* are you among women." With the wonderful opportunity to publish this work, I have substituted Mary's name with my own. God still amazes me with His goodness and mercy that have followed me all the days of my life. How awesome it is to work with Trace Murphy and the Random House/Doubleday family, who understand how to allow me to express and share my blessings in print. Special thanks to Lois de la Haba, my literary agent, who has compassion and wit; to my husband, Ron, and sons, Samuel David and Christopher Daniel, whom God gave to me as gifts; and to the Believers Christian Fellowship Church (BCF), a blessed people, who allow me to lead them. Finally, this work would not have been possible without Brenda Lane Richardson, author and former seminarian, who joined me in prayer, inspired me, and served as a second pair of hands and eyes throughout the writing of this book, whose "gift truly makes room for her" (Proverbs 17), and who has the combination of literary and spiritual genius to bring real stories to life.

LIVE LIKE

You're

BLESSED

How I Learned to Feel B-L-E-S-S-E-D

When I was growing up in Harlem during the fifties, my parents attended different churches, and that made Sundays busy for me and my brother, Charles. First we'd accompany Mom to 137th Street's Rendall Memorial, with its Presbyterian, traditional style of worship, led by our dynamic and handsome pastor, the Reverend Doctor Eugene Houston. He was loved and respected by congregants, and perhaps especially by the children. We'd run to him when we could, bestowing hugs, and reveling in his murmured blessings. Somehow, he managed to deliver inspiring sermons in twenty minutes or less. Closing my eyes, I can still taste Mrs. Bowman's famous strawberry shortcake after Sunday morning service.

An hour later, we were back outside, walking along Lenox Avenue, bound for 145th Street, where Dad ushered at Union Baptist. We knew that once we arrived, we would receive an equally warm embrace from the men and women of the congregation. One of the particular blessings of Union Baptist was its strong male presence. Several of these men became members of our extended family. During the week, many of the men and women worked in uniforms. Sundays were their shine times, when they dressed in sharp suits and freshly pressed shirts, with ties and cufflinks; the women's elegant dresses and suits accessorized with hats and jewelry and gloves. Blessings continued as Dad's pastor, the Reverend Leonard Terrell, delivered stirring charismatic gospel sermons.

Attending two churches was simply what we did in our family, and our full days of worship weren't all that unusual in Harlem. Both of the churches offered different ways of worshipping, but I didn't prefer one place to the other any more than I loved one parent more than the other. We never felt we had to choose. We always knew we had the support of both congregations. We were embraced by two wonderful communities of faith, which are still in my life and ministry today. They truly embody what it means to have church families.

During the walk to Union Baptist, even on cold days, when the wind was like a taunting younger cousin that we had to abide, we might start out with our heads bent, but we knew we couldn't look down for long, not with so many people to greet. I don't mean just giving people a passing nod. Lots of these folks were from the rural south, and had come north during the Great Migration, squeezing into the former neighborhoods of Italian and Irish immigrants. One custom they maintained was getting to know their neighbors. Of course, no matter how familiar with one another, people were addressed as *Mr.* or *Mrs.* or *Miss* by children and adults alike; the titles *Aunt* and *Uncle* being reserved for close family friends.

Because of their long workdays, we didn't see most of these people during the week, but when it became necessary to find someone, these streets were a good place to start. Come Sunday mornings,

Harlem transformed into Church City, with music emanating from run-down storefronts as well as hundred-year-old architectural wonders with towering spires.

Spilling out of residential buildings, spiffed-up adults set out on foot, along with neatly dressed children. This was Manhattan, where parking was scarce and owning a car was more common among the well-to-do. The adults probably felt more relaxed on Sundays than they had been the day before or would be the next. Their jobs, where they were often called by their first names, were still twenty-four hours away. For now their hair was done, apartments cleaned, chickens, and at least two other meats, were salted and readied for cooking. Throughout my mother's lifetime our Sunday dinners were feasts. This was the day to thank the Lord for the week's safe journey.

I've often reflected on the alluring mix of that Sunday Harlem crowd: Baptists, Methodists, Episcopalians, African Methodist Episcopalians and Zionists, Presbyterians, Lutherans, Catholics, Pentecostals, and Holiness. The holiness women were easy to spot by their tambourines, lack of makeup, and long black skirts worn even on the hottest summer days. And Pentecostals had a special way of returning a greeting. When you said hello and asked how they were feeling, they often responded, "I'm blessed." As a child, I heard that phrase so often it became like any other greeting. Many years passed until it changed my life, before I could offer it to others who wanted to change theirs.

With so much church in our lives, you'd have thought that I would drag my feet on the way to Union Baptist. But I didn't, because I knew that Daddy's nephew, Uncle Bob, would be standing out front waiting for us. Uncle Bob had a special connection to our family. Years earlier, when Dad was fifteen, he'd left Prince Edward County, Virginia, because he was anxious to escape sharecropping, an existence he found uncomfortably close to slavery. Two years later, when he was still scrambling to earn a living in New York City, he would send part of his earnings to his older sister, to help raise her three children. With Dad's assistance, one of his nieces, Katherine Cyrus, graduated with a teaching degree from St. Paul's College in Lawrence, Virginia. His two nephews enlisted in the service. When World War II ended, one of the nephews, our Uncle Bob, moved to New York and began attending Union Baptist, which partially explains why he waited for us outside the church.

Uncle Bob and his friends would always hand me and my brother dollars, more than enough to buy two cones of homemade ice cream. Since Dad had provided for Uncle Bob years before, this was his nephew's way of "sowing into us." Before we could finish that last lick of ice cream, we knew Uncle Bob and everyone else would ask, "Where you going to college?" School was a ticket to a more secure life, of course, and he was letting us know that we were expected to attend college. He hadn't had the opportunity himself, and neither had most of the grown-ups in our neighborhood.

My mom, Dorothy Johnson, was different from many of our neighbors when it came to her education. Like her mother, she was college educated. Immediately after graduation from Fayetteville State Teachers College, she'd taught twelve grades in a three-room segregated school in Monroe, North Carolina. Many of the pupils were her cousins. Before long though, she developed an insatiable desire to move to New York. This had a lot to do with meeting my dad, Wilbert T. Johnson.

Years later, I found letters that she'd written to him, with references to the money she'd saved up from a few weeks' worth of wages, sent for deposit in his credit union, minimal sums like $1.47. The two of them were building a nest egg, waiting for the day when they could be together. Meanwhile, Dad worked on his GED. Mom, always the schoolteacher, encouraged his progress, and in one letter, wrote: "Your penmanship is so much better, dear."

Finally, they married and she moved to New York. By then, Dad had become one of New York City's first black trolley drivers, and a few years later, he was trained as a subway motorman. A few blocks from our home, on 144th Street, Mom (along with a dynamic group of black and Jewish educators), began teaching the first of three generations of black children, at P.S. 194, which was called the Countee Cullen School, after the black poet who was educated in New York City public schools before attending Harvard.

Like many members of the emerging black middle class, our family moved to another part of the city as we became first-time home-owners. When I was five, my parents purchased a house in Northeast Bronx, but we didn't get disconnected from our roots. Every few days I paid fifteen cents to hop on the bus and then catch the D train to Harlem, for piano lessons with Ms. Shep, French fries with the girls and the corner store, and to meet mom and her colleagues at P.S. 194.

Disembarking from the train, I often ran into Mr. Tex, a numbers runner, his smooth brown head topped with a tall cowboy hat as he smoked a cigar. Business must have been profitable; he often gave me five dollars, simply because I was Mrs. Johnson's kid. In fact, most of the people on the street recognized or referred to me as Mrs. Johnson's daughter. I'd sit in the back of the room as Mom finished her class, but after a while, Mrs. Carroll, the kindergarten teacher, would ask me to sit in her class too, saying I was a role model for her students. She and other teachers, most of them women, became another branch of our extended family tree. Their graciousness, and that which I received from others, imparted a sense of privilege and protection that made me feel like royalty.

Imagine my shock then, when, after the sixth grade—when I longed to attend the local public school in my neighborhood—my parents insisted on enrolling me in the private Riverdale Country Day school, located in a highly affluent bastion in the Bronx. The $4,000-a-year tuition was a great sacrifice. But, concerned about the cutbacks on services in city schools, my parents grew determined to offer me something more. I got off to a rough start in Riverdale, where I had my first real encounters with racism. For all their mansions and extensive travel, a surprising number of my white, wealthy classmates were culturally ignorant, like the girl who touched my Afro and said it felt like Brillo.

Before long, my parents joined with other black couples, whose children attended predominantly white private schools nearby, and formed a black families association that provided a new group of friends, and eventually dates. I also had a chance to hang out with kids in my neighborhood when I joined a local girls' basketball team.

The alienation I felt at Riverdale continued, however. I only performed marginally well. Then I learned that I'd have to be tutored in English over the summer, because I'd failed to turn in most of the homework. This meant missing out on my regular summer trip to Monroe, North Carolina, where I spent time with my mother's mother, enraptured with her stories about the family and the old days. My grandmother always ended one of her narratives with a parable for life. For instance, she would say, "Suzan, you go back to Riverdale and paint that school black." She was telling me to stand out and make an impression, show my classmates that I came from a family of worthy people.

My school failure was all the more of a disgrace when I realized that my summer tutor was a white Riverdale student, just a few grades ahead of me. I promised myself I'd never be in that situation again. Returning to school that fall, I started earning As and Bs, and in the ninth grade I became the school's first black junior school representative.

That elevated status didn't stop a racist guidance counselor from insisting that I was not "mature enough" to spend my junior year abroad with several of my white classmates in a school exchange program in Spain. When my parents realized they couldn't win that battle for me, they paid for a school course in Valencia, Spain, and sent me over there for the summer. That next year our family traveled together to Puerto Rico, a trip that allowed me to hone my Spanish skills. Two years later, at sixteen, I graduated from Riverdale, and eventually from Boston's Emerson College, at the age of nineteen.

College was great but so was the experience of attending a black charismatic church, St. Paul's AME in Cambridge. Under the leadership of Pastor John Bryant, with the assistance of his wife, Mrs. Cecelia Bryant, St. Paul's became one of the most dynamic churches in Cambridge. There was standing room only on Sunday mornings, as black college students from around Boston swelled the congregation. We were drawn by the holistic ministry that encouraged us to share our gifts while expressing our faith. One young member, who was working on a doctoral degree in physics from the Massachusetts

Institute of Technology, was Ron McNair. Later, he became an astronaut, and sadly, died in the 1986 *Challenger* explosion. Long before that, however, Ron was St. Paul's karate instructor. He'd earned a black belt, and with encouragement from Pastor and Mrs. Bryant, shared his gift with us. As for my contribution, I used my background as a drama and speech major to direct and produce plays involving parishioners.

After years of coping with racism in predominantly white environments, we students appreciated that St. Paul's encouraged us to feel brilliant and black and Christian without apology. Passion can be powerful, especially when people work together in God's name. With an eye on world events, the St. Paul's congregation organized a telethon, WATER, and raised $60,000 for building wells in the famine-plagued African Sahel.

After that, it was no longer sufficient to simply read about the Motherland. Eager to see the continent up close, I volunteered for Operation Crossroads Africa, a program that served as a model for the Peace Corps and that was started by a black Presbyterian minister, the Reverend James Robinson, whom I met through my mother's church connections. I solicited the required participation fees and, immediately after graduation, spent the summer months volunteering in Ghana. It was life-changing to see the land from which my ancestors were kidnapped and brought to America in chains. And something else significant came out of the trip. With no televisions or radios to distract me, I heard God call me to serve through the ministry.

Sadly, my father wasn't there to talk with me about my new endeavor. He died in 1975, during my senior year of college. But heeding God's call, I asked the new pastor at Union Baptist, the Reverend Ollie B. Wells, who was my pastor, to recommend me to the deacons as a candidate for the ministry. I didn't attend their next meeting, but the atmosphere must have been charged with tension. A number of the deacons were in their sixties and seventies, and this was the first time they'd had to decide whether a woman should be allowed to preach. What I do know, is how it ended. I'm told that Reverend Wells reminded the others, "Now, this is Wilbert Johnson's daughter." Partially on the strength of Dad's good name and forty years of service as one of Union's gatekeepers, the deacons scheduled me for a trial sermon. I considered it Dad's last gift to me.

So there I stood in 1980, all of twenty-three years old, the person who used to be that girl out front taking a few last licks of ice cream before the service. The church was packed with regular congregants and my large, encouraging extended family. They waited to hear the young woman who'd gone off to study drama and speech, and in the intervening years had earned a master's degree in teaching from Columbia, and worked as a producer at television stations in Washington, D.C., and in Boston. Now I wanted to preach.

My sermon message was from Paul's letter to the Church at Rome. It's interesting to note that Paul's conversion occurred shortly after he'd finished stoning a Christian and was struck blind. Ironically, the people who nursed him back to health were Christians, and this witness to their faith compelled Paul to change his life. He gave himself over to the ministry. This story suggests that even when we want to resist it, truth can confront us. I knew personally that his call to the ministry must have been humbling, for it required a turning around in an entirely new direction.

My sermon seemed to win over the diehards. I was given a license to preach, and soon afterward, began working on my master's of divinity from Union Theological Seminary in Manhattan, and eventually earned a doctorate of ministry from United Theological Seminary in Dayton, Ohio.

My first parish was an assignment at the Mariners' Temple, a black congregation of fifteen on Manhattan's Lower East Side. Over the course of my thirteen years there, Mariners' grew into two congregations of five hundred each. By the seventh year of pastoring, my life was out of kilter. I'd spent most of my time tending to the needs of my congregation, while leaving none for myself. My efforts to balance my needs with those of others were reflected in two books, *Sister to Sister: Devotions from African American Women* (Judson Press, American Baptist Churches of the USA, 1993) and *Too Blessed to Be Stressed: Words of Wisdom for Women on the Move.*

Following the principles described in the body of my work, thanks be to God, I can say that blessings have continued to flow. In 1991, I married Ronald Cook, who works as an administrator at the Convent Avenue Baptist Church. For him I reserve the highest of compliments: He's a good Christian man. In addition to being a wonderful husband, who takes me dancing and cooks most of the meals, Ronald is a gifted father. Together, we're raising our two sons, thirteen-year-old Samuel and ten-year-old Christopher.

Blessings have continued to flow, including my new church planting position at Believers Christian Fellowship in the Bronx, located a short drive from our home. Ron and I organized Believers in 1996 with twenty-seven founding members, which has grown to include three hundred families. Six years later, in 2002, I was named to a four-year term as president of the Hampton Ministers' Conference, the largest interdenominational clergy conference, representing ten thousand ministers and three million parishioners. Opportunities for public speaking have also multiplied, particularly after I began traveling and speaking with the well-known Bishop T. D. Jakes.

Keeping so many balls in the air has proven to be a challenge. For this reason, I started looking back to my parents' life, wondering what I could salvage from their lessons that would help me serve God, while living my life to the fullest. They were no longer alive when I began this work, but fortunately, I continue to feel their encouraging spirit.

My genesis for illustrating spiritual concepts through storytelling began with my participation, with other African American women from all walks of life, in a group founded in 1998 named Isis, for the Egyptian goddess of fertility and motherhood. Gathering throughout the year, we share stories from our lives that we don't share with others. For that reason, we call it "our safe space" and, thanks to God's grace, we come away feeling emotionally healed.

I pray that you too will find a refuge in these stories. In some cases, the early lives of the people in these stories are marked by what seems a complete absence of hope. In a reflection of the life of our Lord Jesus Christ, they too struggled from the darkness into the light. Their narratives make true that old saying: There is no testimony without a test, no triumph without a trial. Their victories are reminders of the Lord's ability to redeem and restore; His power to help us all lived blessed lives.

With that in mind, I've returned to those Sunday morning crossroads in Harlem, when my family and neighbors remained mindful that no matter how difficult the outside world might be, a deep spiritual reserve could protect us by helping us feel our blessings. With my parents as models, I have learned to live as if I'm blessed. This is not simply something to be mouthed; I've put it into action.

For starters, the word "blessed" is comprised of seven letters, a number that has powerful biblical significance. There were, of course, seven days of creation, and God rested on the seventh day. Seven therefore represents the process of creation as well as completeness in terms of perfection and achieving a goal. Seven is also the number used throughout the Book of Revelation, with its predictions of God's return.

Just as importantly in terms of this book, each of the seven letters in "blessed" offers a suggestion for how to break through the most difficult situations. For that reason, this work is divided into seven parts, with each chapter exploring various aspects about how we can live as if we're blessed.

The *B*—for balance—is a continuation of the messages in my earlier works, which focus on the importance of maintaining emotional equilibrium. My parents, for example, were hardworking people who also knew how to play hard and make time for worship. They also understood the *L* in blessed, which stands for love. This includes accepting the love that flows from God, and extending it to partners, children, and family. *E* for energy is the physical stamina that powers our dreams and helps us to keep on keeping on by nurturing our physical bodies and minding our emotions.

S as in "spirit," is the Creator's power within us, which allows us to serve as God's hands. This reminds me of my father when he was a seventeen year old, sending money back home to help raise his nieces and nephews, and my mother showing up at the end of the day with various children from school, urging them to view our home as a refuge from difficult circumstances. After my mother's death in 2003, I heard from a woman who explained that my parents had helped her pay her law school tuition, and I've since learned of other acts of generosity they extended.

My parents were far from wealthy, but that brings me to the second *S* in blessed, which stands for success. Their wise spending and respect for what they earned allowed them to reach a comfortable level of financial success. To me, success goes beyond an individual's earning power. Financial success empowers us to help others as well.

Thus, it makes sense that the next letter, *E*, stands for encouragement, which my parents certainly practiced. Finally, the *D* in blessed is for devotion to God, which shaped my parents' lives and mine.

I couldn't be more grateful for my parents and for what they gave me, and so I dedicate this book to their rock-solid partnership. To them I say: Dearest Mom and Dad, who are buried together in New York and live together with our Lord in Heaven, I am honoring you through my daily words and deeds. Because of you, I know that I'm blessed. I promise to live as if I am and to help others follow in that path.

Balance

B L E S S E D

CHAPTER 1

Steadying the Seesaw

I heard a story recently about a woman who was proud that she was able to push herself beyond the limits of endurance. And she did manage to get a lot done in the course of the day. But then again, her "day" didn't really end at sundown, or even close to it. In fact, this graphics designer found herself working until 2:30 one morning, and only stopped when she could no longer hold her eyes open. Wanting to have plenty of time the next morning—there was so much to do—she set her alarm for 4:30 a.m. This way, she could finish the work project, get her son off to school, run errands, and take care of household chores.

Just as she'd planned, she was up two hours later, waking herself with a cool shower and mug of steaming coffee. She read her son's homework and convinced him to redo certain sections, while she made him a special breakfast of pancakes. Soon she was waving goodbye to him at the bus stop. Knowing that two hours of sleep hadn't been nearly enough, she scheduled another two at mid-morning and fell into a deep sleep.

17

When she awoke, she figured that some kind of gooey mucus or something had dried over her eyes, because her vision was out of focus. When a warm water rinse failed to do the trick, she started panicking, thinking about all the reasons she needed her eyes, wondering for instance, "How will I see what I want to draw for work? How will I see how to get down the street to pick up my son?"

She started praying, begging God to help her get her sight back. "Forgive me for bothering you," she started. "God I know there are people who have it worse than me . . . people who can't see and can't hear. But please, if it's your will, let me see again."

That calmed her down a little bit, and sometime in the next hour, her vision began improving, but still wasn't back to where it had been. She phoned her physician, scheduled an emergency appointment, but almost pulled a no-show, because she began seeing with complete clarity again. Still, puzzled over why the loss of vision had occurred, and terrified that the episode was the first sign of some terrible illness, she kept the appointment and submitted to a complete physical.

After a full exam, her doctor said he couldn't offer any explanation for her loss of eyesight. The doctor told her she was healthy: great blood pressure, cholesterol, blood sugar. And the temporary loss of vision, he assured her, was not a symptom of degenerating nerves, brain tumors, etc. He added, "I have to admit that I'm stumped."

Grateful and eager to get on with her busy schedule, she thanked the young doctor and was about to say goodbye, when he turned and asked, "By the way, before this occurred were you involved in anything that might have caused you a lot of stress?"

She laughed, and at least that felt good, now that she knew death wasn't imminent. "Doctor, I'm always doing something stressful. Last night, for instance, I was on a deadline, so I only slept for two hours . . . But don't look so surprised. I took another two hours this morning as soon as I sent off the completed job." When he failed to look impressed, she said, "I try to catch up on my sleep on the weekends."

She'd have to do more than that, he told her, if she didn't want to suffer another vision loss. "I think your body was telling you something," he added, and he asked her to sit at a desk and write down everything she'd done in the last twenty-four hours.

After reading over her notes and totaling the number of hours, he shook his head. "If what you're telling me is correct, you worked fourteen and a half of the last twenty-four hours; slept for four; showered, dressed, and made-up in one; four hours were spent running errands and finishing chores, one hour helping your son with homework, and thirty minutes walking here."

He paused, and looked at the woman with a puzzled expression. "Your life is completely out of balance. You'll have to make changes immediately. Your body just told you that, and I don't think it's in the mood to negotiate."

She left, promising him and herself that she'd change her schedule right that moment, that there was nothing that was worth the loss of her eyesight. Walking home, she noticed the trees and people around her. It was late spring in New York City, the rains appeared to be over, and all around her trees were sporting their new warm-weather outfits, bursting with green new life. She even appreciated the people rushing around her, because only hours ago, she'd experienced what it would be like to not see them.

So she thanked God for her vision, and kept taking in the sights, speaking in her head to God, promising that this renewed vision was enough and that she'd never again take her life for granted. "This was gift enough," she finished the prayer. "Lord, I'm not going to ask for another thing, not anytime soon anyway."

With that said, she stepped into the bank to use the automated teller, wanting to buy flowers from the vendor on the corner. But lo and behold, she discovered that her bank balance was zero. What had happened? Had someone gotten into her account and ripped her off? She got out her cell phone and called the bank operator, but got no relief there. It was no mistake, the operator told her. A big check had just cleared, and she gave the woman the number. Yes, she remembered writing that one, but she'd thought she had enough left over to meet her needs. The bank operator advised: "Go home and check your deposits and withdrawals and call us back if you need to. We're here for you twenty-four hours a day."

The woman's steps dragged on the way home, and she certainly didn't feel any better after looking through her bank records, because she couldn't come up with any answer about why the balance she thought was supposed to be there wasn't. "All the other checks I've written will bounce," she thought, and her mind began to fill with ominous thoughts about how maybe this would never be cleared up and how it could be turned into a financial catastrophe . . . The mind works overtime in these situations.

Suddenly, she made a connection: out of balance. Hadn't the doctor used similar words, about being out of balance? This time when she prayed, she dropped her to knees. "God, I just finished saying I wasn't going to ask for anything else, so I'm sorry about panicking like this, but please help me work this out. I can't figure out the message, but I know it's got something to do with balance."

She didn't hear any divine words in her ear, and hadn't expected to, but taking a few deep breaths, she phoned the bank again, and this time she wound up with a bank employee who went out of her way to help. The two of them discovered the problem together. During one of her errands, when this woman was rushing through her busy day, she'd hit the wrong buttons in making a deposit. Rather than $2,400, she'd left off a zero, and credited her account with only $240. The situation was rectified; money was transferred from her savings account to cover today's incoming checks, and she was told that within the next twenty-four hours, the correct balance would show.

Rather than feeling relieved this time, the woman held a finger to her lips, striking a pose of deep concentration as she wondered about the day's theme and what God expected her to learn from it. *Twenty-four hours* and *out of balance*: The words had repeatedly popped up.

"God," she prayed again, "I'm going to figure it out, I promise." Her prayer was interrupted by a call from her daughter, who was attending an expensive private school out in California. The young woman's voice seemed hoarse. "Mom, I'm afraid I have some bad news. I've been in bed for the last few days with a terrible cold. And you know I'm like you, I never get sick. But . . . and don't say I told you so. I've been playing Frisbee. I know you told me I needed to spend any spare time earning good grades, and not waste it with something silly like Frisbee, but I did. And there's this girl on my Frisbee team who always forgets to bring her water bottle, so I've been letting her drink out of mine . . . Yesterday, she told me that she wasn't going to be able to take the finals at the end the quarter, because she has a bad case of mononucleosis: She's exhausted from severe cold symptoms. The upshot is that I think I have mono too, and that means my whole semester may be wasted."

She sounded as if she was waiting for her mother to fly into a rage, but the woman didn't. True, her heart was beating faster at the prospect of her daughter suffering through a long-term illness and falling behind in school. But what she said to her daughter didn't reflect that concern. She said, "I don't blame you for offering your teammate a drink of water after a workout. And if you haven't gone to the doctor yet, you have no way of knowing if you're really sick. If it is mono, we'll deal with it. Now, call me back as soon as you're finished at the infirmary."

While the woman waited for the phone to ring again, she considered calling a client to tell her that she wouldn't be able to make tomorrow's agreed-upon impossible deadline, but she didn't do it, not that moment anyway.

She got back down on her knees and she spoke to God. "I get the message, Lord. I'm not going to start out by apologizing for turning to you. I'm not going to allow myself to feel ashamed for being needy. Things happen in the course of a day and you aren't an eight-hour God, you're there always and at all times. And you're a lot better than a twenty-four-hour teller, because you have my best interests at heart. I'm going to keep coming back to talk to you, praising you for being with me and I'll trust that you'll help me bring my life into balance. The next time I total up my hours, there's going to be more praying. I'm literally going to stop and smell the flowers and do what I need for my body so it can continue to function smoothly. Thank you for blessing my daughter and making her a generous soul. Thank you for the skills of the doctors that are examining my daughter. Bless that woman at the bank who handled my panicky call."

When she'd finished praying, her daughter phoned to say that the doctor diagnosed her as suffering from a bad cold. The young woman would be back on her feet and playing Frisbee in no time. She paused, as if that part, about Frisbee, had slipped out. She knew her mother didn't approve of "time-wasters."

Her mother read her mind. "Honey, I was wrong to tell you not to play Frisbee. I'm so glad you're taking time to enjoy your life. I'm going to start doing the same. In fact, I heard about dance classes at a local gym, and you know . . . your dad and I used to love to dance. Maybe I'll even turn on some music tonight and see if the two of us can remember some of our old moves."

That's right, this woman had a husband, but you wouldn't have known it by her schedule, right? What about you, what are you leaving out of your life?

If you had to write down the ways in which you've spent your last twenty-four hours, how would it look? Try it. Pull out a paper and pen and jot it down. Does your day look balanced? Is there time allotted for resting the body and the mind? Some people need more sleep than others. I call myself an eight-hour woman, and I make it a point to let my friends know. I'm generally in bed by nine and up by five. I've had to learn to make time for all that's important in my life.

When I was a girl, my parents either gave or attended a party every weekend. Doesn't sound like people who sometimes held two or three jobs at a time, but they managed to do the work, raise us, party with friends, save their money and invest it, and attend church. At one point in my life, I lost sight of maintaining that kind of balance. Even my soul was weary.

Since then, the many strategies I employed for alleviating my spiritual, emotional, and physical lethargy have been shared with thousands of men and women, from all walks of life. I have traveled the country talking with those who are seeking hands-on practical advice for managing their lives and tools that will help them create a measurable difference. I've spent more than a decade helping others pursue their passions and dreams. Often, in assessing our lives, we realize we have not devoted enough time or thought to our own passions, plans, and pursuits.

As the Balance Doctor, I am always trying to find ways to help people realize their dreams and live the lives they truly want. They begin by learning to balance their lives by holding on to a mental image of the seesaw. I use this familiar childhood playground favorite, the seesaw, because everyone can relate to it.

Often, a picture of scales is used to connote balance. But I believe that down time, recreation, and play are important aspects of the "dream life." In the park, the seesaw is more than a piece of wood that goes up and down. It teaches children that if a balance isn't struck, they will not have a smooth and successful ride. Too much weight on either side causes one end to go up and the other down. This is true in life as well. Too much weight in life causes our stress indicators to go up, our health to go down; our blood pressure up, our spirits down. Our lives require balance.

I have learned to borrow a page from my parents' lives. Recently, in fact, Ron and I hired a sitter and danced the night away to our favorite seventies songs. And because life is so circular, decades earlier and a few blocks from where we were clapping our hands and moving to the melodies, Ron had been a teenage member of the Afro Gents dance group, helping to get more than a few parties started. He's still a smooth operator. More than that, he's my playmate; the partner who helps keep my seesaw balanced. We all need that kind of lover, or friend, or relative, or perhaps a spiritual advisor, someone to depend on who will be there for us during life's many ups and downs. Remember the seesaw ride when the ride was going smoothly until the other person suddenly leaped or fell off? You went slamming to the hard ground and that felt pretty miserable. That's why you need to seek reliable, prayerful support.

Can you recall a recent time in your life when perhaps a physical symptom, financial loss, or alarming phone call sent you crashing to the ground? Of course, life happens, but there's a way to spend more of your time maintaining an even keel.

I can just hear the protests. "I've got work to do," or "Who's supposed to bring in the money while I'm playing on that seesaw?" I understand the skepticism. Let me assure you, I believe in the benefits of hard work. And no matter what kind of work you may be doing, including volunteering, it's good for the soul. We should all work and contribute our gifts. As Big Mama, one of the characters in Brenda Lane Richardson's *Chesapeake Song*, points out: "Everybody's got to work. Even a broke clock give the right time twice a day." The catch is that you'll work more efficiently if your life is balanced.

I've included tips on how to move beyond the guilt that's churned up as we make time to create balance in Chapter 2. For now, try the following visualization.

Sitting in a comfortable position in a quiet spot, where you can breathe easily and deeply, imagine waking up on Christmas morning. See yourself descending a wide marble stairway and hearing a loving, joy-filled voice greeting you: "Good morning. Oh, just wait until you see what I have for you. There's so much I want to give you."

You exchange warm hugs and kisses and, as you sit, you're handed your first brightly wrapped package. You pull off the wrapping, and the figure eight drifts out, which makes you ecstatic. "Eight hours," you say. "I have eight hours."

You're imagining what you can accomplish in all that time, and like almost everybody at Christmas, in the back of your mind, you're wishing there was another gift to open. And there is: The next package actually contains another eight hours. The eight floats up, undulating in the air and you laugh at its playfulness, assured that now there's time to add fun to your list. You feel rich in time. And you are.

And because God always gives us more than we ask for, there is still another box under the tree. And, you guessed it, it contains eight more hours!

As you continue visualizing, you hear your favorite music playing. You jump up, the shining eights bouncing and twirling as you dance. What a day of gifts! You embrace your time and promise your gift-giver, who is the Holy Spirit, that from this point on you'll spend the gifts wisely. With a deep, cleansing breath, open your eyes.

Using your favorite pen and taking your time, write a list of what you want to "purchase" with your gifts of time. Work at changing your perspective by remembering the wise words of poet and Nobel laureate Rabindranath Tagore: "The butterfly counts not months but moments and has time enough."

Since you're not rushing, take the time to write in a penmanship that reflects you at your best. Write your list as if you were communicating with someone of great importance, because you are: This list is for you. If you start by listing rest, recuperation, sleep, exercise, and meditation you may find that these set just the right tone for change in your life. Then there's work, of course. (Hopefully you're engaged in a career you love. If not, I'll discuss that in detail, later in this book.) What else is added to your list? How about chores? Regular responsibilities, like cooking dinner, shopping, helping the kids with homework. Remember to leave time for spontaneous events—like calling a best buddy and asking her to meet you for dinner and a laugh-filled conversation.

As you compile your list, whenever you find yourself panicking about how you'll get it all done, go back to that place at the foot of the Christmas tree . . . feel the gift. Thank the Creator and remember to keep your spiritual account balanced.

Prayer for the Day: *Dear Heavenly Father, you have given me so very much that I am wealthy beyond measure. Thank you for the hours of the day and the sense of purpose I carry that has been passed on from my ancestors. Dear Lord, help me to remember that your wristwatch doesn't necessarily run at the same speed as mine, and that your time is the highest authority. With your help I'll keep an even keel, sailing my ship of life. Above all, I will remember that right at this moment I am exactly where I'm supposed to be. All things in your name, Amen.*

CHAPTER 2

Eliminating Guilt

The young woman had made an appointment and as soon as she was seated in front of my desk, and the door closed behind her, she collapsed into sobs. It took awhile to ferret out the reason for her distress as she continued by moaning about having to pay for her selfishness. With gentle probing, I learned the cause of her anguish. Her husband of two years was having an affair, and he blamed her. "He's tired of coming home to an empty home and empty bed," she explained.

This twenty-something, childless parishioner was an up-and-coming business executive and during the previous year had spent a lot of time on the road developing her career. As her tears subsided and we continued talking, I learned more about her so-called "selfishness."

Every Friday, even when it might mean the loss of a potential client, she flew back into town early enough to prepare dinner for her husband, so they could start the weekends off right. And she kept Saturdays sacrosanct, always reserving the day to join him for his favorite sports events, even when she would have preferred to take some down time or get her hair done at a favorite beauty salon. During her weeklong absences, she often phoned him and sent him romantic notes and occasional gifts.

Maybe you're thinking (as I was) that she sounded like an exemplary wife, so I wondered why her husband was blaming her. And how had he managed to turn the tables and make her feel guilty? The truth is that no one can *make* us feel guilty. They might attempt to, but their manipulations won't work unless life's experiences have made us prone to feeling guilt.

Exploring the issue of guilt is of particular importance here, because it can get us off balance and keep us there. If the goal is to maintain a state of equilibrium—remember the image of the seesaw and the laughter it evokes—then guilt could well be described as dead weight. This young woman didn't have any children who needed her time and attention. She'd been intentional about building her career before having children, hoping that later, when and if she became a parent, she could have more flexibility and travel less. And she was clearly making an effort to shower her husband with love. Why should she feel guilty about having to be out of town for work or ignore her own needs?

Don't get me wrong. A modicum of guilt can be healthy. There aren't many pastors who won't agree. Righteous guilt is an inner alarm that God designed in humans to tamp down our arrogance and help make us moral beings. Those feelings of unease and that flush of discomfort remind us that there are some things that we really should—or should not—do. It's not necessary to enumerate those "shoulds" and "should nots": They were written in stone and can be found today in Exodus 20. Of course I'm referring to the Ten Commandments.

As a pastor, I've found that women tend to experience generalized feelings of guilt that have to do with societal expectations about the female role; about nature and nurture, and the fact that during childhood most girls are given dolls to rock and tend to—early training in how to devote ourselves to the needs of others.

The most damaging form of guilt is that which is passed on in families, when parental figures harshly scold children for making mistakes and blame them for their misfortunes. I'm thinking about a well-meaning single father who took on an extra job to pay for his son's Catholic school tuition. Unfortunately, when the boy brought home a failing grade, his dad angrily listed the sacrifices he was making so the son could get a good education. Although the boy hardly listened when his father said, "I'm proud to be your father and blessed to be able to give you a good education," he did feel profound guilt during his dad's scolding lectures. In fact, he started hating that he was enrolled in a school that was so expensive that his dad was exhausted and broke trying to keep him there.

The guilt the boy felt interfered with his learning. He was disappointed in himself, and finally admitted during one heated family session that he spent all his extra time playing computer games and talking on the phone, rather than doing homework. Furious with his dad for humiliating him when he failed, the boy was unintentionally trying to get back at him by failing. It was a clear example of guilt standing as an obstacle to a balanced life. The boy taking time for play and socializing was great, but his life could have been more balanced if his guilt and anger hadn't caused him to fail.

A lot of adults struggle with guilt long after childhood, especially when it stems from memories of parents favoring one child over another. Some of these favored children suffer with "survivor's guilt." One woman from Kansas, I'll call her Paula, has a life that many would envy. She's an active Christian, happens to be physically beautiful and healthy with a sunny disposition and, after a first marriage that ended in an amicable divorce, Paula became independently rich.

Despite her comfortable life, Paula struggles with survivor's guilt. Her two sisters have lived through great misfortune, and whenever they call for loans—which is often—they constantly remind her that their parents didn't love them as much as Paula. Not for a minute am I discounting the grief these women feel. In too many families, especially in the past when there was less information available about the emotional needs of children, parents often showed favoritism. The grief these sisters felt was probably genuine.

But here's the catch. Guilty feelings are out of control when we feel responsible for the happiness, comfort, safety, and peace of mind of those we love. It's an impossible task, and yet, when we don't live up to it, guilt leaves us feeling helpless, remorseful, and powerless. Time after time, Paula has flown to different cities to bail her oldest sister out of legal troubles stemming from her drug use, and she has footed the bill for her to enroll in several rehab programs, which have proved unsuccessful. The youngest sister has her share of troubles in choosing the wrong men. Paula has rushed in trying to save her, too.

Paula is a perfect example of someone struggling with what I call the Savior Complex. Of course people like her don't think they can handle supernatural tasks, but they do feel they can make everything better for those they love. But allowing loved ones to work through their own problems, saving themselves, actually gives them opportunities to mature and feel more confident. When we insist on trying to alleviate a loved one's suffering, that loved one may take us for granted or treat us with contempt.

A few years ago, for example, Paula was ill, but when she called to ask for support, her sisters didn't return her phone call. Paula recognized the connection between her deteriorating health and the guilt she felt about her sisters and turned to a therapist for help. In creating a balanced life she has learned to say no to her sisters. Not surprisingly, they were furious with her. In fact, one of them called her a selfish bitch.

When you try to bring your life into balance and make your needs a priority, don't be surprised if some of the people who are closest to you respond in a negative manner. Children and siblings, friends, husbands, boyfriends, parents—the list can be endless—won't want you to pull back in providing for them. As theologian H. Richard Niebuhr has pointed out, the first law of humanity is self-preservation. No matter how much we may pride ourselves on our independence, in our hearts we all want to have someone who will place our needs above their own.

In creating balance, we focus on that which helps us feel nurtured, while maintaining clear boundaries: understanding about where our responsibilities end and where a loved one's responsibility for himself begins. And we learn to decipher the difference between *feeling* selfish and actually behaving in a selfish manner.

My female biblical role model is Deborah, who I consider the first real multitasker. A wife, prophetess, and judge, Deborah was a woman with clear boundaries and high self-regard. She took pride in her respected position in the community—one of the other people who rose to her level was Moses. And talk about intriguing work! As a judge, she got to make decisions; as a prophetess, she remained attuned to God's desires.

It was an enormous job, but rather than running here and there to hold court with the Israelites who turned to her for help in settling their disputes, she sat beneath a tree that was named for her—the Palm of Deborah—and people came to her.

At some point, Deborah told a man named Barak that God commanded him to assemble ten thousand warriors and confront their enemy. When he responded by saying he wouldn't go unless she did, she agreed to accompany him, but first she reminded him that he wouldn't get all the credit for her work. She said there would be no glory for him in victory, because the Lord would be delivering the Canaanites into a woman's hands.

Deborah was right: They won the battle in an overwhelming victory. And today, Deborah is known as the Mother of Israel. Something tells me she didn't spend a whole lot of time feeling guilty about reaping her well-deserved glory.

Another of my role models, my mom, did feel somewhat guilty about not always being around when I needed her. After we moved to the Bronx, Mom had to manage the household on a fairly rigid schedule. Dad left for work on weekdays at 4:30 a.m., long before we awoke. About an hour later, Mom rose and got dressed and was in the car by 7:15 for her drive to Harlem. The infrequent mornings when she was still around and I was attending a neighborhood elementary school, she walked me about a block, kissed me goodbye, and prayed that I'd arrive safely. Most afternoons, when I wasn't taking the train to Harlem to meet her, I was a latch-key kid and went home to an empty house.

Several of the homes of our Italian-American neighbors were more traditional. Many of the mothers stayed to home to cook, clean, and care for younger children. There were times when I wished for a similar lifestyle, and years later, I told my mother, "I wish you'd been around to brush my hair."

My mother responded without bitterness, "Honey, I did the best I could do."

How gracious of her not to snap at me and remind me of how much she'd done for me. Any sadness I felt about not having more of her in my young life was mitigated by a life-changing experience. I became a mother.

I remember waking up that first day, at the hospital. I'd slept deeply, following an epidural. Ron had left the room temporarily and Mom was standing over me.

My first words were, "Did you see my baby?"

"I saw your baby and he's healthy, beautiful, and fine."

Before the day was over, she was cradling Baby Boy Samuel and showing me how to feed him, hold his head, and change his diaper. She kept kissing and kissing him, wanting him to know that he'd been born into a loving family.

I have two sons now, and know what it's like to have to balance their needs and mine, without letting my guilt take over. We all do the best we can.

During a recent speaking engagement in Atlanta, someone offered me a luscious dessert, and although I would have enjoyed it, I turned it down, and confided to a friend that my favorite desserts were my husband's still warm, fresh-from-the-oven banana pudding and my son Samuel's yellow cake with chocolate frosting. Hours later, when I returned home late in the evening, I found a note taped to the front door.

"Hi Mom, please go to the kitchen. There's something you like in there."

As if he'd read my mind, Samuel had baked a yellow cake with chocolate frosting. Savoring a healthy slice, I sat in our sleep-hushed home, feeling too blessed to feel guilty.

Battling Guilt

- If you're a parent, start a purse-sized notebook for each of your children, and when work requires you to be away, write a short entry. It might be something as short as, "Oakland, Calif., Jan. 16th, here for consultation. Wish you were here to laugh with me about the nasty pancakes room service delivered. Miss you, Mom." Let your child read the notebook when you return home, and continue writing. Over the years, this will become a valued keepsake.

- It is also important to plan great vacations when you're away a lot. For example, when I recently returned from leading the Hampton Minister's Conference, I had planned a family vacation—an eight-day family retreat in the Bahamas—so we could have uninterrupted time together. Since the boys heard that I'd stayed in a "Royal Suite" it was important to them for them to have similar accommodations.

- Parents also find that it helps to relieve guilt if they make it a point to praise children for skills they may have learned as a result of them not being there. Maybe a child learned to do laundry because a parent didn't have the time to handle that chore. When you praise your child for a job well done, point out that he is making it easier for you to support him.

- E-mail is a great connector for parents who are often away from home. If you subscribe to a service with parental controls, you'll have more peace of mind when you encourage your child to IM or e-mail you.

- If you know you're going to miss a lot of your child's school events—plays, games, recitals—find a parent that does attend regularly and offer to share photo processing expenses if he or she takes pictures of your child as well as his or her own. Be sure to display photos of your child in action—on a refrigerator, office desk, as your computer's wallpaper.

- If you have to break an engagement with a loved one, send them an IOU. Say "This is good for one_____" and fill in the blank: basketball game, concert, lunch out. Make sure you honor your heartfelt debt sometime in the near future.

- Stave off feelings of guilt concerning a romantic interest by finding creative times together during the day. One woman used to meet her husband in the lingerie section of an exclusive department store, and after they purchased something he wanted her to wear, she made it a point to find a time when she could model it for her. Another couple takes "poetry breaks": via telephone, by reading lines from Rita Dove, Langston Hughes, or excerpts from other favorite poets. Another variation on this is the share-a-joke calls.

• If you have a friend who often feels guilty about being away from a child or spouse, host a "praise party" for her. Invite her closest friends and family and take turns telling her why you think she's wonderful and why she's important to you.

Devotion: *Lord, thank you for giving me this day my daily bread. I have not accomplished all that I wanted to, but for what I have accomplished, I give you thanks and glory. I praise you for the spirit that kept me going. I've done my best today. Please let me sleep peacefully and begin tomorrow fresh and ready for that which awaits me.*

CHAPTER 3

Spiritual Balancing

Given New York City's outrageous traffic, with cars moving in fits and starts, creeping along and then picking up speed, cabs veering into different lanes and jaywalkers darting between cars, a lot of residents refuse to drive. I'm not one of them. I don't like taking cabs or letting someone drive me. When I'm alone in the car, I'm in control. I know back streets, and there's always the challenge of creating new routes. I'm an aggressive New York driver, and when I'm alone in my car, I'm working out my stuff. By the time I get to where I'm going I've chilled out.

This doesn't work for me when the tires on my car need balancing. After a winter of bumping over gaping potholes, the steering wheel begins to vibrate, and after awhile I have to take the car in to have the tires balanced. The technician mounts a tire on the balancing machine and spins the wheel to locate the heavier part. By the time he's finished and I'm on the road again, I'm pleasantly surprised at how much smoother my car rides, and then I'm back in control, behind the wheel.

There's a parallel between feeling in control behind the wheel and feeling in control in life. Just as I'm intentional about taking my car in to have the tires balanced, I have to approach life with the same sense of purpose.

Moving through life is the issue. We are powered by God, who is within us. Yet, he has blessed us with free will. He doesn't move us around like puppets. He gives us the freedom to love and obey him. The goal, then, is to keep our lives balanced so we can discern God's purpose and distinguish between what we want and what He wants for us: God's perfect will.

I have four different approaches to spiritual balancing that you might find helpful, all of them involving prayer. When it comes to praying, the equation is this: much prayer, much power; little prayer, little power; no prayer, no power.

Fasting

For me, personally, prayer in conjunction with fasting has proven to be a powerful combination. Some people think of fasting as a modern fad, but of course it dates back thousands of years. Perhaps one of the most memorable fasts in the Bible is undertaken by Jesus when he was in the desert for forty days. "He ate nothing during those days, and at the end of them he was hungry" (Luke 4:2). To Satan, who tried to tempt him, Jesus responded: "Man does not live by bread alone, but on every word that comes from the mouth of God" (Matthew 4:4).

Jesus's single-mindedness and focus was enhanced by the spiritual discipline of fasting, for it serves a number of functions. As a ritual, it has a humbling effect, reminding us of our neediness. It is also an act of devotion that subjects our will to the will and wisdom of the Holy Father. His will and wisdom are more easily discerned because fasting gives us more time for praying and listening, when we might otherwise be taking time for meal preparation and eating. And finally, fasting is an act of emulation, showing God that we too are willing to suffer for the greater good.

In 1991, after ending a disappointing relationship, I wondered about my future. I'd pastored a church for eleven years and had discovered that since leading a church was such a new role for women, a lot of men viewed me as holy, unapproachable, and untouchable. Not many men were comfortable in the role of the pastor's boyfriend or husband. That meant I had an additional challenge because I would have to be in an unusual holy alliance. I felt that if it was God's will for me to remain single, I was certainly willing to accept that. If it wasn't, I'd already had enough of heartbreak and heartache, and I didn't want to move into another relationship blindly. I wanted help in finding the right mate and felt that fasting would help me discern God's perfect will.

There are no rules or standards for fasting. Dietary approaches always work best when they're based upon an individual's specific health. In my case, after getting medical clearance, I began a forty-day fast, ingesting liquids during the day and having one meal in the evening. During that time, I prayed to God, asking for clarity and focus concerning my romantic life. My fast began in January and lasted into February. This wasn't the first time I'd utilized this tool, and as before I found that cutting down on food became easier with each passing day. As excess weight dropped from my body and my cells were cleansed of toxins, I began to feel energized.

A month later, on the Monday of Holy week—which that year began in February—I attended a conference at Convent Avenue

Baptist Church in Harlem. At the end of the day I was greeting one of the pastors, the Reverend Fran Manning, when out of the corner of my eye, I noticed a handsome African American man in a well-tailored suit.

I asked Fran if she knew who he was. Raising an eyebrow she watched him for a minute and then turned back toward me with a smile. "That's Ronald Cook, our church administrator, and I think he's single."

I'm not generally very assertive when it comes to meeting men, but this time I practically insisted that she invite him to join us for dessert at Copeland's Restaurant, where we planned to dine, and he quickly accepted.

The entire time the three of us sat in that busy Harlem eatery, Ron and I kept making eye contact, and as soon as Fran went to the bathroom, it seemed he and I couldn't stop staring at each other. So I was pleased when he said, "I've always wanted to meet you." He admitted that he'd always thought of me as unapproachable.

I was thinking, "I've always wanted to meet you too." I'd seen him before from a distance, but this was our first time talking. What I'd heard so far impressed me. His job as Convent's administrator required him to understand the rigors of a pastor's duties. He was also religious, intellectually curious, and a good listener, and he had a great sense of humor—and did I mention he was good-looking?

Later that evening, it was just the two of us, sitting in his parked car on 125th Street, hurriedly exchanging biographical details. Ron had been raised on 144th, the same street where I was born, and, like my parents, his hailed from Virginia and North Carolina. All of that could have been written off as coincidence, until he added, "I've just finished a fast."

I almost gasped when he said this, and grew more astonished as he continued. "I asked God whether I was ready for marriage. If you are the woman God sent to me, I promise to be a good steward over this gift."

Enclosed in his car and hearing these words, I felt I was about to embark on a holy alliance. I was deeply moved as he added, "Let's leave it to God to confirm. Why don't we fast again for another forty-eight hours and then talk?"

I know now that it was love at first sight. From the time I saw Ron at church, it was as if I had always known him. We saw each other that next Wednesday and then practically every day thereafter. By June we wanted to get engaged. First, though, Ron wanted to ask some special people in my life for permission to take my hand in marriage: my mother and my favorite aunt, Katherine—one of the nieces from Virginia that my dad had helped support and put through college.

My mother had already grilled him on several occasions, and as far as she was concerned he'd already passed her stringent test. Aunt Katherine gave an enthusiastic response, and pulling me aside, she whispered in my ear, "He's a good man. Be good to him. Don't chase this man away." Only weeks later, she died and I never again saw her alive. My mother, however, lived for many more years and took Ron to her heart, like a mother to son.

The moral of this story is not that fasting will lead you to the life you desire. Jesus's life certainly wasn't a bed of roses after he returned from the desert. But fasting did prepare me to become more engaged with my spiritual life. And for all I know, submitting myself completely to God's will softened my body language or added luster to my skin, thus making me more attractive to my future husband. You'll remember me saying that before our meeting Ron had viewed me as unapproachable, but this time he hadn't. And this I know for sure: The discipline of fasting prepared me to be more open and trusting and reawakened my bruised heart. Like the saying goes, chance favors the well-prepared.

Visualization

There's another romantic story I'd like to share, about a woman who prayed and asked for discernment, utilizing a slightly different approach. Lee's two-year marriage had disintegrated and she was troubled at having to raise a son without an involved father. She became very intentional about the kind of balanced life she hoped to create.

"Maya Angelou has said that if you want to know about a person, you only have to listen and he'll tell you all about himself," Lee says. "That couldn't have been truer about my husband. When we met, he told me he was a Christian, but that he didn't go to church. I didn't challenge him because I was happy to have someone who loved me. I settled for less.

"Once we were married," Lee continues, "serious problems surfaced. He kept a mistress, stayed out plenty of nights, spent lots of time in bars, and beat me if I dared to complain. That was when I realized that just saying you're a Christian doesn't mean much. I could say I'm a bumble bee, but I can't fly or collect nectar from flowers because I'm not a bee. I wanted to live in a home and be part of a team of two Christian parents whose faith could be seen through their actions. But I could never appeal to my husband on moral grounds, because he felt whatever he did was acceptable, as long as it didn't land him in prison. He had no moral basement. He just kept getting lower and lower. I knew that this was a long way from the life I wanted, and I made him leave."

Distraught, every weekday morning Lee began going to a chapel located in the church building where she dropped her son off for preschool. "I went faithfully, and spent about a half hour each time on my knees, praying and visualizing the kind of man I needed. I wanted someone who could be a good father for my son and a faithful husband to me. I didn't picture any physical characteristics, but I merely asked God to send me someone who walks his faith. I kept visualizing a man who was literally walking, bathed in God's light. I wanted a Christian marriage."

Worried about Lee's sanity, her friends asked her about her long prayer sessions in the chapel, and she assured them that she was growing stronger by the day. About a year later, she took a business trip to New York with a coworker. When she was rushing from her hotel room for a meeting, her coworker admitted that he was attracted to her and she grew outraged. "I don't know why his confession infuriated me, but he had a creepy personality." She went to the meeting as scheduled, but midway through, began feeling terrible about the way she'd spoken to this coworker. Leaving abruptly, she sought him out and apologized.

"He accepted my apology, and knowing I was familiar with the city, he asked me to take him to Grand Central Station, where he was meeting a former roommate for lunch. I didn't want to go, but I'd acted so ugly earlier that I wanted to make it up to him and I consented."

They stood in the middle of busy Grand Central Station, and Lee turned her gaze toward the flow of busy tourists and commuters, rushing toward trains and subways. "At some point, I saw the face of a tall, handsome man. I got only a glimpse, but that nanosecond was long enough for me to notice that he was wearing a clerical collar. I thought, 'Okay God, that's the kind of man I've been praying for, someone who walks his faith.' At that point Lee says the man looked toward her and her coworker. "He began waving at us, and the closer he moved in our direction the faster he walked."

The friend her coworker was meeting was an Episcopal minister. They exchanged numbers, and after a few years of dating, he and Lee eventually married. Over the next fifteen years Lee's husband and her son had a turbulent relationship, but today her husband and son are close.

"When things got rough between the two of them, my husband could have thrown up his hands, said 'He's not my son,' and walked out, but he didn't. He stayed because he's a good man with a conscience and when we took our vows he knew the deal included my son. Staying was the right thing to do. My son got the message from watching him that a real man doesn't walk away from obligations. Now he has grown into a man who honors his promises."

There are no scientific explanations for the events in Lee's story. It's true that researchers have found many instances in which people have focused on an image, and given it lots of positive energy until it became an objective reality. But there's no need for a scientific explanation. Through the frequency of her prayer Lee aligned herself with He who governs the principles of the universe, our Great Creator, the Lord God.

Writing Letters to God

Few things can make parents feel more desperate than out-of-control teenagers. When children are little and don't follow orders it's easy enough to just lift them up and carry them to wherever you want them to be. But if they act out when they grow up, life gets more complicated. The rage and fury generated between parents and children can throw every member of the household off balance.

John, the father of a teenage son, had always said that if his son didn't obey him he was either going to put him into the street or kill him. Fortunately, he didn't overreact when his son was fourteen and was arrested for shoplifting.

"When the call came, I was like one of those parents on TV: 'Sorry, officer, you must have the wrong number. My son is upstairs doing his homework.' "

But there was no mistake; it was in fact John's son. John gave him a stern warning and grounded him for a month. "He started sneaking out at night, after my wife and I went to bed."

More arrests followed, as did angry confrontations and attempts to handle the situation with "Tough Love."

"When we received another call from the police station and heard that my son and his friends had stolen someone's car keys, I told them they could keep him in lockup." John's wife begged him to let their son return home, and for a while things seemed to be improving, especially after the young man went into therapy. "I was willing to try pretty much anything," John says. "I felt shell shocked. The two of us had once been very close. Things cooled down around my house."

Not for long. The young man quit therapy, stopped going to classes, and his parents found marijuana in his room. "He heard I was looking for him, and he didn't come home for three days. In the middle of the second night, I was combing the streets for him when

I ran into one of his youth pastors. She advised me to go home and start writing letters to God. What else was there left for me to do?"

John wrote long impassioned letters to God, pouring out his grief, asking how things had come to such a sorry state. At the end of each letter, he thanked God for keeping his son safe and asked him to help him calm the anger between the two of them.

"I have a box full of those letters. For the next year my son was in and out of the house, but I didn't ask him to leave and I kept writing."

Years passed and the box was put away, and then one afternoon John ran across it at the top of a closet. "I reread the letters and was dumbfounded at how bad things used to be between us. I suppose I forgot because we lived through his rebellion. He served in the Marines and he's over here all the time now, with his wife and children."

I've found that often when we ask God to intervene in a difficult situation, if the change doesn't occur very quickly, we forget to acknowledge the blessing. John's letters may have had a hidden benefit, providing him with an emotional release that mitigated some of his anger and made it easier for his son to approach him. If you decide to write letters to God, you may enjoy entering them in your journal.

Assembling a Prayer Group

The woman, a writer, had been working on a particular manuscript for three years, and time and time again she met with disappointment. She received rejection letters from thirty agents, but whenever one of these communications contained helpful advice, she incorporated changes into the manuscript and then sent it out to different agents. After two years, she found an agent who liked her writing enough to submit the manuscript to editors at major publishing houses. Two weeks before the submissions, she wrote to twenty of her most prayerful friends and asked them to pray for her.

"I didn't ask them to help me get a lot of money," the writer explains. "I asked them to pray for my peace of mind, because I knew I would be sitting on the edge of my seat while the editors were looking over my manuscript, and I asked them to bless the editors who would be reading it." Her friends wrote back with assurances of prayer.

Five editors received copies of the manuscript. "It didn't take long for my agent to call and tell me about the first rejection from an editor, who said I didn't write well. Of course, I was disappointed." The second, third, and fourth rejections caught her by surprise. "One claimed it moved too slowly. Another thought I should cut out references to faith. Another said he was sure I'd sell it, but not to him." News of the fifth and final rejection was swift in coming.

"I heard my agent's voice on the phone and I said, 'Don't tell me. She's not going to buy it.' My agent agreed that I was right, but added, 'There's some good news. She says you're very talented. She loved the book and just wants you to make some minor changes.' "

The writer is now back at work, making revisions in the manuscript. At this point, she still doesn't know whether the editor will buy it. But she says of her prayer group, "Their encouragement and support has allowed me to rewrite with a renewed vigor. I've pursued this dream for a long time, and I was exhausted. Those rejections from editors, especially comments about me not being able to write well, might have put me out of business, but I'm at it again. My friends continue to send me encouraging notes that I treasure. Their prayers are keeping my battery charged."

Remember that image of taking a car in for servicing, when the technician mounts it on a rack so he can balance the tires? Well, this is the human version of balancing. Good news or bad, the writer will emerge from this experience with a community of friends willing to stand as his or her partners in Christ. If you're facing a difficult situation, you might consider asking friends and family for support. They'll keep you lifted up through prayer. What a positive way to develop a sense of balance.

CHAPTER 4

Coming to Ourselves

As we continue to explore the *B* in Blessed, under the subject of spiritual balancing, it's important to consider the story of the Prodigal Son (Luke 15). In this narrative, the son takes his inheritance from his father and goes off to enjoy a dissolute life, squandering his money. When he realizes his mistakes, he returns home and is welcomed by the father. This symbolizes our relationship with God, who offers unconditional love. He is always willing to forgive us, no matter what our sins.

For the purpose of completing our discussion on creating balance in our lives, it is important to home in on one particular verse in the Prodigal Son's story. It is the passage in which the son seems to awaken from a drunken stupor: "And when he came to himself, he said, How many hired servants of my father's have bread enough and to spare, and I perish with hunger" (Luke 15:17). The hunger of which he speaks is the need for something substantive in his life. Now, ordinarily, I wouldn't think it was wrong for a son to ask for his inheritance and strike out on his own. I encourage people to seek out new experiences. But this is not just any Father and child, this passage is about breaking away from God. A second offense is the son's squandering of his inheritance. An inheritance isn't something that we earn; it is a gift, and thus, this story is about not misusing the gifts that God has given us. The son makes mistakes, as most of us do, but more importantly he eventually "came to himself."

Let's look closely at that phrase and the meaning behind it. It seems he finally recognized his own nobler attributes, which were his greatest inheritances and which could not be accounted for in a bank ledger, aspects like self-respect, love, gratitude for family, and obedience to God.

After a time of drunkenness, coming to oneself represents a moment of great sobriety. The prodigal repented. And repentance is a decision followed by appropriate action. He realized he would prefer to be with his father as a slave than alone amid the fleshpots of the city, and he returned home.

This moment in Luke is tremendously important for those of us striving for balance. In Part I of this book, we have learned why striking a balance is important, moved through the guilt that might prevent us from attaining it, and learned how to utilize tools that can help us enjoy balanced lives. But it's impossible to move on to the next step, if, like the Prodigal Son, we are not spiritually ready. If we are not ready, we will allow our gifts to be squandered. If we are not ready, it won't be necessary for a robber to take our gifts away from us by force—we will hand them over of our own accord.

This is a lesson played out repeatedly in the media. Consider all the Hollywood celebrities who supposedly have "everything," including talent, good looks, fame, mansions, and multimillion-dollar bank balances. All this allows them to acquire anything they want, when they want it. And yet, so many of these celebrities appear on television talk shows, or in courtrooms, or write tell-all memoirs detailing their squandered lives. They aren't the only ones. Think of the many political leaders and corporate executives who seemed to have it all, but come to admit they have so little. They are glitzy reminders that we must come to ourselves before we can savor the taste of the fruits on our Father's vines.

Whatever happened to the Prodigal Son? Once the party his father threw to welcome him back had ended, did he spend the rest of his days making up for his lost time? Did he strike it rich or forget what he'd learned and once again head for greener pastures? It doesn't say, and there's reason for that. It's not what Luke wanted us to focus on. In writing this story, he was pointing out that as long as we breathe, our future, like that of the Prodigal Son, remains open to possibilities.

When I consider possibilities, I think of a young woman, who, for the sake of anonymity, I will call Linda. Unlike the Prodigal Son, Linda was not born into prosperous circumstances. In fact, Linda was raised in Miami by a teenaged mother. "She was only fifteen when she met my father," Linda says. "He was twenty and had just arrived from the Dominican Republic. He reeled my mother in. I was her first child and I have five siblings under me." Her father eventually went to prison on drug charges and she saw little of him.

"When I was little, I used to wonder why my mother exuded such anger toward her mother. My grandmother was young too. After she moved to Miami from Georgia, she started having children at fourteen, and she had eleven of them—five from her husband, who was sent to jail and then never returned home, and six kids from a boyfriend. My grandmother was the type that hung out, partied, and drank with her kids. She liked having a good time.

"I later learned that her boyfriend had raped my mother, and when my mother explained what happened, my grandmother called her a liar. She must have believed her though, because she stabbed her boyfriend with a knife. He stayed around after that for many years until he died. Fortunately, no pregnancy resulted from the rape."

Linda's mother, a victim of this man's violent behavior, became angry and overwhelmed with the responsibilities of raising her own children and turned to drugs. "When I was eight or nine years old, my mother would take me to her friends' broken down rooms and I was her protector. I'd have twenty dollars tucked down in my panties to make sure we had money to get home after her drug spree. I'd watch her shoot heroin into her veins. She got money from welfare. When she had four kids and was pregnant with twins, I started begging her to let me go along when she cashed the checks. She'd say, 'No, bitch, I'm the grown-up here, I'll take care of it.' I knew if she didn't take me along to the check cashing place, she would go off with her friends and get high, then we'd have another month with barely anything to eat."

With so much turmoil at home, attending school regularly was difficult for Linda. "Especially because my mother was physically abusive," Linda continued. After an angry argument with a boyfriend, when Linda was about nine, her mother called her and a younger brother into her bedroom and asked whether they thought she loved them. Before they could respond, "She beat the hell out of us," Linda said. "I thought she was going to kill us. She hit us with her fists and with any objects she could grab. She punched and scratched my face. I'd fall and she'd say, 'Get the fuck up, bitch.' She ripped my brother's T-shirt and started on him. I grabbed him and ran and we hid under a bed."

When Linda showed up at school the next day, one of the neighbor's daughters, Emma Jean, invited her to their home. Once there, Linda confided in her classmate about her mother's abuse. "I didn't realize that Emma Jean's mother, Mrs. West, was listening outside the door. Mrs. West scolded Linda's mother about the abuse and took Linda to church, where the young girl found comfort in the idea of a loving Father.

Life only grew harsher for Linda and her siblings. "My mother died from AIDS when I was sixteen. My grandmother had already raised eleven kids and she was resentful about having to take us in, but there wasn't anyone else." The grandmother pressured Linda to drop out of high school and get a job. Linda did quit, but she ran off with a man who was ten years her senior. He rented a furnished room for them in Delaware. "I figured now I could create a better life for myself and then help my brothers and sisters."

That better life never materialized. As psychologists often point out, a lot of people re-create situations in their new lives that are reminiscent of the ones they left behind. In Linda's case, that meant drugs and physical abuse. Her new boyfriend free-based cocaine and he beat her. When Linda tried to leave him, he doused her with gasoline and tried to set her on fire. Her life was spared when his cigarette lighter failed to work.

Returning to Miami to escape him, Linda discovered that her oldest brother was selling drugs. She moved in with her grandmother, determined to help support her other siblings, and found a job as a manager at McDonald's. Before long, she met Alfonso, a police detective, the man of her dreams. "Talk about awesome!" Linda enthuses, and adds, "try fantastic, wholesome, the epitome of a good man. I kept waiting for the other shoe to drop. I was sure he'd tell me he was gay or he'd turn on me and beat me."

Five years her senior, Alfonso turned out to be protective and gentle. "He was the youngest child in a middle-class family. His parents worked for the city. They're stable people who spend holidays and birthdays together, enjoying each other. My experience with family gatherings had been people getting drunk, fights breaking out, and seeing blood. Alfonso's family showered him with affection. He'd had some trouble in his past. When he was younger, someone offered him coke and he took it and got hooked. But his parents hung in there, made sure he got treatment, and he joined a twelve-step program."

After two months of dating, Alfonso took Linda to meet his family. She watched with awe when he spotted his mother returning home from a shopping trip and rolled down the car window and called, "Hey Mama, where you going, beautiful?" Alfonso parked, hugged his mom, and insisted on pulling her grocery cart. "When I saw that show of love, I was blown away. That was the day I thought, Oh, God, I love this man."

Like many people who have experienced childhood trauma, Linda unconsciously tried to drive Alfonso away. "By 1991, we lived together. One day I came out of the shower with a towel around me, thinking Alfonso was gone. But he was at the desk paying bills. I thought my body was too heavy and ugly to be seen, so I asked him to leave the room so I could get dressed. When he resisted, I said, 'Get the fuck out.' "

Instead of leaving in a rage, Alfonso told her, "'I'm not leaving. I don't know where you're coming from, but I won't entertain it.' I was still in fighting mode, so very gently, he pulled me to the mirror. He said, 'Have you looked at yourself? You are so beautiful. Anybody would want to look at you.' I repeated, 'Get the fuck out of the room.' He told me, 'I love you, but you still don't trust me.' He pulled the towel away from me, and oh, my God, my worst fear was feeling vulnerable. But he made me look in the mirror. He said, 'Do you see that woman? I love everything about her. You're beautiful. Even if you had five stomachs I'd love you. I want you to be my wife. I know we have many enemies out here, but I'm not the enemy. Stop trying to ruin our relationship.' From that point on, I felt I could fly. I thought, 'This is it. I'm covered. I'm protected. He loves me for me, fat or thin, stupid or smart, progressing or digressing. He simply loves this person.' "

The two married soon afterward, started a successful security business, and purchased a five-bedroom home. But by Christmas of 2001, three months after September 11, 2001, Alfonso was struggling with the sense of helplessness that plagued so many officers in the wake of the attacks, a situation that was compounded by recent arguments with his ex-wife over seeing his eight-year-old son for the holidays. To Linda's great dismay, Alfonso began using drugs again.

"I got hold of him at work. I was livid. He'd stayed away all night, and I said, 'Alfonso, what are you doing? We've got a lot going for us.' He talked to me about the drugs, how they were like a demon. 'I can't seem to fight them,' he said. That night, when he didn't come home, I knew I'd never see him again."

She was visiting Alfonso's sister when the police arrived. They said he was sitting in a parked car and had died from a single gunshot wound to the head. "It was suicide. I felt like somebody had robbed me."

There was a $100,000 insurance settlement, but Linda ran right through that. The business she'd built with Alfonso failed and she was unable to maintain the mortgage payments on their home. "I moved to Philadelphia, wanting to get away from the memories. I started asking God, 'Why did you let this happen to me? I'm scared and I'm standing in this world all alone.' For years I was like a zombie. I worked as a receptionist and lived a quiet life. I didn't have anybody. I didn't think I had God either. I wasn't getting any answers and I was just about ready to give up on Him."

At some point a niece phoned Linda and convinced her to accompany her to a church service in suburban Philadelphia. When they arrived, Linda learned that the guest speaker was Bishop T. D. Jakes. Linda had read about him and was moved by his powerful sermon.

When he finished preaching, Reverend Jakes looked out at the congregation, and announced: 'I came all the way from Dallas, Texas, because there's someone out there that God wants me to talk to. I know you think you're here by accident, but God knows you're on the brink of giving up. He said to tell you, don't give up, that he has a plan for your life. Whoever that person is out there, all you have to do is stand and come to this altar. But first you have to believe that your new life is getting ready to happen."

I and a few others went down to the altar. Reverend Jakes looked me in the eyes and said, 'Don't give up. God is at your door. Don't you even think about giving up.' "

Linda said that moment marked a turning point. "From that point on, I decided to live my life on purpose. I thanked God for seeking me out, and I am so grateful that there is still breath in me. I do have a protector, someone I can rely on. And that person is not a man or woman. All that can pass away. God's love is forever." She says her new attitude made her work more enjoyable and she stopped dragging through the days.

I've shared Linda's story because her moment of realization, when she came to herself, is an important one. Many of us may have different details to our stories, but we have also experienced pain and disappointment, and I want you to know that God has not forgotten you. God, who only acts for the good, has a better life awaiting you.

Finally, there's a last important point I'd like to make about the Prodigal Son. When he returned home, his father didn't just look out the window and say, "Well, he's coming back. I knew it." No, he made no attempt to hide his joy at the son's return. In fact the father ran outside to greet him. That is God's grace. As in the story, our Father says: "What happened before no longer matters."

If, like Linda, you feel lost and weary, take comfort in knowing that God seeks you and awaits your return. The Holy Ghost is relentless and will never stop seeking you out.

If you don't belong to a church now, I urge you to join one, attend, and confess your faith. As Linda learned, if you haven't invited God in, make room, because He is just outside your door; He is simply waiting for you to come to yourself.

PART II

BLESSED

LOVE

CHAPTER 5

Loving God Back

I n the preceding chapter we were reminded of how blessed the Prodigal Son was to have a father who offered forgiving and restoring love. By extension, we too are blessed because that loving Father is our God, as known to us through Jesus Christ. Hallelujah! Glory be to the Father, and to the Son, and to the Holy Ghost. Amen, Amen. Amen. If you think I'm smiling, you're right. Moving on to the *L* for love in "blessed" makes me think about the Lord's love, and that makes me happy. It puts me in the mood for a party or two and gets me chanting: Ain't no party like the Holy Ghost party, and the Holy Ghost party don't stop.

I've got to stop myself right now—no easy task, because I'm blown away by the power of God's love. After all, it was from the abundance of divine love that creation spilled out. That's right. God didn't *have* to create us. He didn't create us out of *necessity*. We are the products of the overflow of God's love, and we love God back. Don't we?

Well, let's think about that. What does it mean to *say* we love

God? That's an important question when you consider that we often say what we don't mean. If someone greets us in the morning and asks, "How are you?" even if we're dragging in the depths of our soul, we usually respond, "I'm fine, thank you." We might not mean it, but we want to be civil.

And our polite but perhaps not genuine kind of responses don't necessarily end with salutations. Think about a job interview. Maybe someone has grilled you, and left you feeling a bit inadequate and unsure about whether you'll get a hoped-for position. When it's time to go, you might extend a hand and say, "It was good to meet you." No big deal, a mere utterance. Sometimes these kinds of words reflect our true spirit and other times they are merely polite ways of communicating with a new acquaintance.

Some words, however, are reserved for the most intimate of relationships, and "I love you," is one of them. Those three words are serious. They raise the stakes. If we say "I love you" and don't mean it and our actions contradict it, the listener might feel betrayed, and rightly so. We hear the word "love" quite often in songs and read it on greeting cards and hear actors on television and in films say it aloud.

These are expressions of love between human beings. That's different from the love we accept from and offer to God, according to my spiritual advisor, Dad Mason. To much of the world, this vibrant eighty-three-year-old is the Reverend Doctor Elliott James Mason, Sr., a former Fulbright fellow who served for twenty-three years as the pastor of the three-thousand-strong Trinity Baptist Church in Los Angeles.

"When people fall in love with one another, whether they admit it or not, they're usually expecting something in return," says Dad Mason. "Unlike humans, God doesn't deal in percentages. God doesn't ask for fifty percent. God's love for us never diminishes. He loves us even when we don't give anything back. It's unconditional love."

But when we say, "I love you too, God," we're talking to someone who, whether we live or die, we shall not be separated from. That's why loving God back calls for a personal and total commitment, the kind that's discussed in Luke 10:27: "You shall love the Lord your God with all your heart, and with all your soul, and with all your strength, and with all your mind; and your neighbor as yourself."

Just in case we missed the part about the neighbor, Jesus continues by explaining the story of the Good Samaritan, who showed extreme compassion to a stranger. Jesus isn't a halfway kind of savior. What he was saying is that action speaks louder than words. If you want to show me how much you love me, then love your neighbor.

You might remember Lee, whose stories are woven throughout this book. When she and her family moved to New York City, she thought she'd prepared her children for every kind of contingency. They'd lived in California, in an exclusive suburb outside Oakland, where doors were left unlocked and, from their front door, her children walked barefoot if they liked, down to a pristine playground where, at the end of the day, fathers were rolling up their shirtsleeves and teaching their sons how to hold baseball bats. The weather was often so perfect year-round, they called it Garden of Eden weather; the streets were safe, the houses luxurious. They lived in that neighborhood through God's graciousness. Someone from church owned the property and kept the rent low so Lee and her family could afford it. Lee's family thought they'd be there forever, where the neighbors were pretty easy to love.

But Lee's husband, a minister, was called to a new job, teaching seminarians in Manhattan, and the family left the easy life behind. After the pristine, homogenous environment they'd known in California, New York City was a little intimidating, to say the least. But they were prayerful people. Lee figured that if she taught her children to be street smart, the rough edges of their new life could be smoothed out.

Determined to teach their children to love the Lord with all their heart and soul and strength, the couple made time for their family each morning before heading out to work and school. They huddled in a circle, their arms around one another's shoulders as they thanked God for their blessings and asked Him to help the children get over the grief they felt about leaving behind friends and comfortable lives.

As had become their practice, once the last amen was said, Lee's husband took their twelve-year-old son uptown by subway. In the afternoon, the boy rode home with classmates. One morning, before walking out of the door with his dad, the boy looked over at Lee. "Mom, when I'm on the subway without a grown-up, all these homeless people come over to me and ask for money and ... well, they're so dirty and ... they smell so bad. I don't know what to do. They scare me."

Getting ready for work and not wanting to hold the boy and his father up, Lee said the first thing that came to mind: "Whatever you do, if one of those men asks you for something, don't answer, don't make eye contact, and walk away."

The door was almost closed when the boy poked his head back inside. "But Mom, what if one of them is Jesus?"

The question haunted her the whole day long. She couldn't risk her son's safety. He couldn't give money to any stranger that came along. But the boy was right. How did her message jibe with what she'd taught him about the Good Samaritan and about loving our neighbors as ourselves? If it was true that God was in every one of us, those men on the train were no different. But she'd told her son to turn his back on God.

By evening, she'd worked out an answer. She apologized to her son for brushing him off that morning and told him that his question had been a good one, the kind she needed to hear. "I'm not backing off on the warnings. Don't take unnecessary chances. It's not a good idea to speak to strangers. But how about this: Once a month we'll have bake sales in the lobby. You and I can bake on Friday evening, and on Saturday morning, we'll set out a table and sell the goods so we can give the money to the homeless."

The boy loved the idea. That was five-and-a-half years ago. He's seventeen now, but they're still hosting bake sales. Year in, year out, calling out to passersby, "Cinnamon rolls and blueberry muffins; red velvet, coconut, carrot and lemon cakes; chocolate cookies and ba-nana bread." The two of them—mother and son—have become quite a fixture with their folding card table. And the hundreds of dollars they've raised over the years have been donated to a local men's shelter, buying food and blankets, and one year, a Christmas tree.

As is true of all volunteer work, it's not just the recipients of the charity that profit. Lee and her son have remained close even during the typically difficult adolescent and teenage years. In fact, in that same spirit, that boy—now a young man—is preparing to go to

Kenya for the summer as a member of a relief team that will help construct a school for children whose parents have died of AIDS. That young man will spread word of God's love through example. As Dad Mason says, "The only way we know we're returning God's love is when that love flows through us to others."

He is so right. Loving God can change your life. The more love we give Him, the more He gives back. It's the gift that keeps on giving.

Loving God back is not something we can do by following the numbers. God is always challenging us to do more. Coming to know and accept Jesus is for us the very essence of discipleship. It's about undergoing a radical transformation. Consider the story of the rich young man who obeyed God's commandments, but who was told by Jesus: "Go, sell what you have, and give to the poor, and you will have treasure in heaven; and come, follow me." When the young man heard this, "his countenance fell, and he went away sorrowful; for he had great possessions."

This passage is often invoked by me and my fellow pastors to remind Christians of the importance of tithing as a religious duty, but as is always the case with our Good Book, there's more beneath the surface. That story is about submitting to God's will. That means allowing the Holy Spirit to guide our prayers, hearts, tongues, minds. That passage is about total commitment, moving beyond self-centeredness to being God centered.

This deep level of commitment requires more than weekly devotions. Some people think that going to church on Sundays is sufficient. They may think, "I sinned this week, but I'm going to church, and I'll ask God to forgive me." God is always ready to receive us, and although He does appreciate our efforts, He by far prefers steadfast love over sacrifice.

Loving God back is a twenty-four-hour-a-day commitment; it doesn't end because we're busy or feeling stressed. That's what a woman I know reminded herself after a long workday. Before going home, she rushed into a supermarket, grabbed a chicken and, with growing impatience, stood on a slow-moving line and listened in outrage as a surly cashier lashed out at customers. "I couldn't believe the way people allowed her to intimidate them. She snatched money from them, sucked her teeth if someone asked a question about a price, and she tossed their change on the counter. People were shaking their heads and commiserating through eye contact, but no one stopped her. By the time she got to me, I figured she deserved a good scolding. When my turn came, and she gave me one of her nasty looks, I said in a voice that carried: 'Oh, I've got it. You're pretending to be the world's rudest cashier, because there's a hidden camera under there. This is some kind of reality show, right?' "

The cashier blushed beet red, and her eyes grew moist as she said in a tremulous voice, "I'm sorry. I've had a terrible day."

The customer later said, "I felt terrible for her and I regretted allowing myself to react like a bully. People like that cashier are almost always miserable."

Maybe you're thinking, That girl deserved that and more. No matter what her problems, she should have left them at home. On one level I agree. We can usually find an excuse for un-Christian responses. And perhaps for women of color who have an ancestry that involved servitude, humbling yourself in the face of withering contempt is not an easy discipline to master. The next time you're in a similar situation, it might help to envision yourself towering over the rude salesclerk, or whoever seems determined to ruin your day, and seeing yourself as having been made larger by God, who's lifting you up. This can help you walk away without the nasty verbal payback, still your tongue, and allow you to respond to who this person truly is—probably someone hurt and broken.

Seeing differently is part of the radical transformation that we undergo in giving love back to God. If you were raised to envision God as a shaming, hectoring, angry, and disapproving father figure, know that this is more of an outgrowth of your childhood experiences than the reality. A lot of people believe that God punishes people by allowing terrible calamities to befall them. But as Dad Mason reminds us, "We can't blame anything bad on God. Humans may commit evil, but the very nature of God's movement is to rescue us. God is nothing but goodness."

One of the most important passages that supports Dad Mason's point can be found in Romans 8:28: "In everything God works for good with those who love Him."

Because we are among those who love Him, let's conclude by thinking of someone we've known, whom we loved quite deeply, but who is no longer with us. Maybe it's a mother or father or grandmother. Whoever this person might be, concentrate on someone who worked hard and didn't receive the glory he or she deserved.

Now imagine getting a phone call and hearing that this person has actually come back to life and is going to be celebrated for his contributions. You've been invited to join the crowd and wave and cheer when he passes by. At that point, you arrive at a ticker-tape parade, just in time to see the person you love passing in a car, with the convertible top down. You're so grateful to this person for all he has done for you, and your cheers mingle with those of the others in the crowd. You wave your hands and call out, "I love you. Thank you for all you've done."

When it's over, you think, "Isn't it funny, the crowd was so large and yet I felt that he saw me. But even if he didn't, I was just glad to be there to say thanks."

A little later, when you run into a neighbor and she asks you where you've been, you explain that you've just left church. Because that's what church is, joining with others, taking part in the thanking and praising when He is in our midst. Because we know that actions speak louder than words, attending church is one more way to express: "I love you too, God." You're loving God back.

CHAPTER 6

Healing Shame

We're still exploring the *L* for love in "blessed," so let's consider what might happen to make us stop loving ourselves. You've heard of all-purpose cleansers. Well, toxic shame is an all-purpose blocker. Like a high wall that keeps sunlight from penetrating into a room, toxic shame blocks out self-love because it keeps us unaware of the various gifts God has given us. Toxic shame is so powerful and packs such an industrial-strength wallop, that even if our lives are filled with abundance—including God's love, good health, a rewarding career, and a comfortable income—toxic shame will block us from living like we're blessed.

Guilt, which was examined in Chapter 2, is very different from shame. Both are painful, but guilt is connected to behavior. The discomforting flush of guilt is caused when we have not lived up to our own standards or values, or have hurt someone we care about. Adam and Eve almost surely and deservedly experienced terrible pangs of guilt. Their sin wasn't about biting into an apple, explains the retired New Testament professor William J. Richardson: "Their sin was that they sought to establish their lives on their own terms apart from God, while using the gifts God had given them. They were trying to be like God." Fortunately, God allows us to atone for our sins. As such, guilt can be mitigated by changing our behaviors or attitudes.

Shame, on the other hand, is personal and insidious. It makes us feel that *we* are wrong and that no matter the extent of our achievements, we aren't good enough and never will be. Though we might be the honored guest at a posh celebration, shame can make us feel as if we're dressed in rags and that we're inadequate, phony, failures.

Everyone experiences shame; it's only human. But shame can build up in some people until it reaches toxic levels and becomes corrosive, eating away at a person's healthy self-image. People suffering with toxic shame are so busy trying to hide their sense of inadequacy that their behavior becomes exaggerated. Instead of radiating self-confidence, they are contemptuous of others. Instead of offering helpful advice, they are controlling or self-righteous. Instead of enjoying one drink they may have many—often *way* too many. Compulsive behavior usually shows up in one form or another, including eating and indebtedness. Instead of buying a nice outfit, for instance, this person may buy a closet full of clothes and overspend until there's no money left to pay the mortgage on a much-cherished house. Another image that pops up for me, as I think of squandering God's gifts, is of inmates in long-term confinement who didn't become great mathematicians, or lawyers, teachers, doctors, artists, historians, or whatever because—just as someone can be "high" on a drug—they were "low" with toxic shame and made terrible choices.

Acknowledging shame and asking God for help are certainly important first steps in healing. Unfortunately, too many people have had their faith derailed by self-righteous people who used religion as an excuse for abusing them. All of us know people who were "whupped in the name of the Lord." Their parents might have whaled away at them, reminding them on each down stroke that "God don't like ugly."

I'm not talking about a mild spanking, but physical or verbal abuse, which is degrading and dehumanizing. These children may grow up filled with toxic shame and feel estranged from God, if the parent claimed that he or she was acting on God's behalf. Although the parent or guardian may have whipped a child under the guise of making him or her "walk right with God" this treatment can actually have the opposite affect, estranging the individual from God. And once the covenant is broken, an individual can begin to feel numb inside and act shamelessly.

One of my closest friends, who for the sake of privacy, I will call Frank, is a pastor at a thriving Baptist Church in Tennessee. Frank grew up in Atlanta, with five siblings, in a home headed by two hardworking parents. His mother was a registered nurse, and his father was employed by the city.

"My father was co-owner of a liquor store," adds Frank. "And unfortunately, he was his own best customer. He was what you call a functional alcoholic because he kept a job and earned a good living, despite his abuse of alcohol."

What his father couldn't control was rage, and some of Frank's earliest memories are of his father beating his mother. "My sisters and brothers were fearful when they saw this occurring, but I was the child that my father said had 'too much mouth,' and I didn't remain silent. I'd try to protect my mother, and my father would turn on me. One time he pistol-whipped her and I beat him with a hammer."

Frank was too young to overpower his father. "I took the brunt of the beatings, and these went beyond the norm. Once a belt was deemed insufficient, I was beaten with boards, broom handles, whatever was in reaching distance."

Although friends and relatives advised Frank's mother to leave her husband, she refused, on the grounds that marriage was a sacred bond that should not be broken. "It was clear from observing my parents that there were two ways to go in life: the way of the light or of darkness. My mother was the epitome of a saved person. She prayed for my father and believed her prayers would save him. And she knew that when sober, he was among the best of men. Unfortunately, he was rarely sober during my childhood and he often came home in a drunken stupor."

Despite the father's misbehavior, he demanded that his children follow the highest moral standards. "I was a little bugger," Frank recalls. "I'd lie about something, nothing catastrophic, but my father couldn't stand for me not to be truthful. When I was about nine or ten, I bullied a little boy and took his money, and lied to my father when he asked me about it. My father went through my coat pockets and found the money. He felt beating me wasn't getting him anywhere, so he tried psychological abuse."

His father picked up the phone and pretended to call the police, saying that he wanted his son taken away. He packed the boy's clothes and told him to get ready to go. His sisters and brothers sobbed and begged their father, "Please don't let them take Frankie away." At this, Frank says, he broke down and began crying. "My father discovered he could torment me with psychological abuse."

School became a refuge for Frank, and he excelled academically, skipping two grades. At the age of fourteen, during his sophomore year, he was called by God to preach. "I was pretty focused about becoming a preacher and serious about school. The worse things became for me at home, the more it drove me to prove that I could be better than my father. I was undaunted."

By sixteen, during his senior year, when his father threatened him with another beating, Frank moved away and rented an apartment. After high school graduation, he worked full time at a local factory, while attending college full time, striving for an undergraduate degree. "On the afternoon work shift I had a certain quota to meet, and for the first hour and a half I'd get ahead of schedule, then I'd go into the bathroom. I'd hidden my textbooks in the garbage can when I first arrived, and that's how I got my studying and homework done, sitting on the toilet, my feet propped up, hiding in a stall." One of Frank's supervisors noticed his long bathroom breaks and asked him if he had a problem. "I told him yes, I did. I'm lucky he didn't ask me to elaborate."

Through graduate school and while working on his doctoral degree, Frank continued supporting himself, proud that "I didn't have to ask my father to buy me as much as a pencil." Over the years the two men have reconciled. Frank's father has stopped drinking and apologized for his past cruelties, but some pain isn't easily diminished.

Frank's academic life continued full tilt, but at heart he was still that little boy who'd been beaten like a mistreated farm animal. Desperate to numb himself from his shame, he became a womanizer. "I looked mature for my age, and I was about thirteen or fourteen when women began exploiting me sexually; some were from church. I thought their special attention meant that I was special. I started believing that sex was just a way of expressing myself. From my perspective it made me more of a man. In this society, the guy with the charisma that gets the girls is seen as the one with machismo."

His sexual promiscuity occasionally got him into trouble, and caused at least one near-death encounter. A Vietnam vet, disappointed upon returning home to hear that his girlfriend had been unfaithful, "phoned me at my mother's house, and said, 'Listen, man, I was right outside your church today. You didn't see me because I was across the street with a rifle. I saw your head through the scope . . .'"

Frank now says, "That definitely encouraged me to give the woman up, but she kept pursuing me."

Frank knew that he was hurting the women that he slept with and then casually discarded, but he now realizes that he wasn't the only one acting out his shame. Many of the women seemed drawn to him because of his misbehavior. He continued using sex like a drug. His shame made him believe he would remain that way forever.

Despite the changing faces in the lineup, Frank maintained a relationship with a longtime steady girlfriend, Anne. "She was so innocent, my mother loved her. I occasionally brought different women home to meet my parents, and a lot of them were very impressive, but my mother would tell them, 'You're a wonderful girl, but do you know my daughter, Anne?' "

His mother insisted that Anne was the woman he'd marry. "It was true that I always loved her, and somehow, even though she knew I was acting up, Anne remained supportive and prayerful. She never ranted and raved, and she never had another man in her life. Anne believed that God would change me."

One demonstration of her faith in him was that Anne quit college after two years so she could help him continue, and she gave him most of her $3,500 savings. "I realize now that I was re-creating my parents' relationship of light and darkness."

When he was twenty-six, Frank married Anne. "With God's help, I put that womanizing life behind me," he says. Knowing that shame only festers when you try to bury it, he opened up to his wife and others about his childhood abuse and his own adult wantonness. One of his favorite sayings is, "By reconnecting with who you are, you can redirect who you are; it's connection with direction." He adds, "When you get right with God, you're right for everyone else."

A few years later, he was leading a church, building membership from eighty to eight hundred. He and Anne have two teenage daughters and two grown sons who are enrolled in law school. He and his wife also own a thriving restaurant.

Frank's past still weighs on him. When asked to imagine what he'd say to the women he slept with and then deserted, Frank's rich baritone voice faltered. "I would certainly say that I'm sorry, sorry for corrupting and reducing the value of your worth. I treated you like objects. What I did was not worthy of you or God. I'm sorry that I made you part of my ugly reality. And I urge you not to set-tle for anybody who will make you feel less than you're worth."

Frank encourages people with similar childhood experiences to speak out about what they suffered. "Don't hide your past, don't act as if terrible things haven't happened," he tells the young people of his church. "Use your past honestly and let God help you redeem it."

Listening to Frank's story reminded me of men that I've known who hurt me. When I emerged from a relationship feeling mistreated, I felt shame. In seminary, I dated a fellow student and we were talk-ing about getting engaged. When I started pastoring at Mariners'

Church, parishioners grew accustomed to seeing us together. But the relationship ended abruptly, because that was his wish. It left me reeling. I felt vulnerable and exposed, because I was the one who had to keep explaining our breakup, even though I didn't really understand the reasons myself. Maybe you're going through something like that now, and if so, I'm sorry. I remember how much it hurts.

That was one reason I shared Frank's story. I hoped by understanding his past you would see how many people—men and women—bring their own brokenness to their relationships with others. Even when you can eke out a little sympathy for the person who hurt you, you may wish he could offer you an explanation.

That's what happened to Brenda Lane Richardson. "James was my first boyfriend," she says. "I was fourteen, and I still have a faded photograph of me sitting with him on the grass, during our first and only date. It's obvious from the way I'm staring at him that I adored him. I can remember our first kiss and that he told me he loved me. A few days later, when I called him, he hung up the phone. I dialed again, and for the second time he hung up. I couldn't fool myself anymore. He'd dropped me like a sack of dirty laundry. When someone does that, you're so embarrassed; it's as if your body lights up and everyone's staring right through your clothes."

Thirty years later, James and Brenda reconnected. "I was speaking at the National Association of Black Journalists, in Atlanta, and was surrounded by a group of people when a man approached and said, 'You probably don't remember me.' Without missing a beat, I said, 'Sure I do. Your name is James, and you broke my heart.' He was astounded that I remembered him." When Brenda explained that she was happily married with three children, James seemed pleased. He said he'd heard she was speaking and that he'd driven from Florida to see her.

He said, "I'm in Alcoholics Anonymous and I'm making amends to the people I hurt. When I hung up on you that day, it was partially out of cruelty, but it was also to protect you. Our house was insane. It made me reckless and angry and I knew I was bound to hurt you. But I hurt you anyway, and I'm sorry."

I commend James and Frank for their honesty and for their willingness to change. How about you? Have any of your childhood experiences led you to hurt others or yourself? In your journal, write a letter to an adult who hurt you when you were a child. The idea isn't to blame that person for your troubles nor does the person have to see the letter, but naming him or her and detailing the experiences are a good start toward healing the shame.

When you have finished writing, close your eyes and visualize yourself unearthing a treasure chest. You open it to reveal precious jewels and glistening gold coins, which upon closer examination are the gifts God has given you. Take a deep breath and describe those gifts aloud.

When you have finished speaking, open your eyes, and know with perfect assurance that the harder you work to uncover the experiences that caused you to feel shame, the closer you come to recognizing and utilizing your gifts from the Creator. In coming weeks, continue to write in your journal, join a support group, or seek out therapeutic help if necessary.

As you repeat the buried-treasure visualization you will find that your list of gifts continues to grow. Like a flower sprouting and then bursting open in sunlight that recognition is your growing self-love. I'm tempted to close by saying God bless you, but He already has. Your task is learning to give expression to those blessings.

CHAPTER 7

Learning to Love Yourself and Others

In the preceding chapter, I explored the ways shame blocks self-love, but now we need to consider why self-love is so important. When I was growing up, loving yourself wasn't something that was considered positive. Back then it had a different connotation. If someone said, "He's in love with himself," that suggested the selfishness and self-absorption of a narcissist. You know the kind of person I'm talking about. He or she might inquire about some problem you're going through and instead of sympathizing or coming up with a solution starts thinking about how he or she will be impacted by your troubles. They won't want to be inconvenienced. Bet you know someone like that. Believe me, I've been there.

Another belief system that contradicted the need for self-love was the notion of agape, self-sacrificing love, as practiced by God. Of course He demonstrated His love for us through the death of his son, Jesus Christ, which allowed us to be reconciled to Him: This is the most important message of the Bible.

The question then becomes, how do we as Christians *dare* to love ourselves? But it also stands to reason that if we believe that we are created by God and in His image, then it is our responsibility to love ourselves. This is not simply a fuzzy, feel-good idea. Loving ourselves as God loves us allows us to sustain ourselves through hard times. Our inner well of love is created by serving God—and by that I mean loving God back—and benefiting from positive childhood experiences.

So many times in my life, my heart has swelled with gratitude at the memory of my parents sitting spellbound as I read to them aloud in Spanish. They understood that the world was growing into a global village and they worked extra jobs to earn enough to send me to Spain and take our family to Puerto Rico, so I could master the language.

Those parental looks of admiration and other experiences, like my Uncle Bob waiting outside Union Baptist to remind me that I was smart and had to go to college because I was representing the family, those infusions of love and confidence filled me with self-regard. When the hard times came—for instance, that almost-fiancé of mine, calling it quits and leaving me to explain to others why he was gone—I had to tap into my inner well for reassurance. That, and knowing that God was with me, helped me get through it.

But what happens when the well is dry? Maybe you had hardworking parents who were so focused on the necessities of your survival that there was little time or energy for demonstrating the kind of love we all require. Toni Morrison, one of America's greatest living writers, brings home that point in her novel *Sula*. In one scene, Hannah asks her mother Eva—who literally sacrificed a foot to support her children—whether she ever loved her. Eva's response is bone-chillingly to the point.

You settin' here with your healthy-ass self and ax me did I
love you? Them big old eyes in your head would a been two
holes full of maggots if I hadn't . . . Wasn't nobody playin' in
1895. Just cause you got it good now, you think it was always
this good? 1895 was a killer, girl. Things was bad. Niggers was
dying like flies . . . What you talkin' bout did I love you, girl.
I stayed alive for you, can't you get that through your thick
head.

This scene makes clear how love can be viewed from two completely different perspectives. Eva felt that keeping her children fed
and housed was a sufficient show of love. But Morrison demon-
strates that Eva's inability to show motherly affection didn't preclude
Hannah from needing it. For that reason, Hannah doesn't survive
long after this conversation. It is as if Morrison is reminding us that
we don't live by bread alone. We need love, and that includes self-
love.

Taking a look at the quality of your relationships may be the best
way to gage self-love. In the last chapter's discussion of toxic shame,
we looked at the exaggerated behaviors that can be adopted as defenses against shame. Consider how contemptuous behavior, for instance, can drive people away. It is the same for angry outbursts,
self-righteousness, and a host of other negative behaviors. That's
why toxic shame and self-love can't coexist within our psyches.
Working to lower toxic shame is an important first step in learning
to love yourself.

Journal writing and prayers continue to be of critical importance.
Men may feel more comfortable with a spiritual guide (ask your
pastor for recommendations). As you write or speak about painful

memories, which may include abandonment and abuse, your soul will begin to feel lighter.

Then comes the important job of learning to take care of yourself. If you have a history of mistreatment, of course you have learned to devalue yourself. So it's important to begin providing for yourself the way you would your own beloved child. That may sound strange, but the truth is it's often easier to care for others than it is to care for ourselves.

For instance, there are certain things that you might want to keep your daughter from experiencing. Maybe she has a boyfriend that neglects her and runs around with other women. You would almost surely counsel her to move on, and tell her that she deserves better. To treat yourself lovingly, you may have to follow some of your own good advice.

Developing a nurturing internal voice is a challenge, but an important one. To illustrate that point, I want you to stop a moment and think about what you need right now for the rest of your day to feel more balanced. I asked that of one woman, who said, "I just want to take a shower. I've been so busy getting this house clean that I was afraid to stop. The kids will wake up in a few minutes and I need to have my work finished."

When I pointed out that her actions suggested that it was more important to mop a kitchen floor than to give herself a few minutes relief under a warm and soothing shower, she realized what I meant. She added that she'd fire a babysitter if she neglected her daughter that way. This is why acting as our own good mothers is so vital in learning to treat ourselves lovingly. The more we act on our own behalf, the more we love the person we're fighting for.

What do you need to do for yourself right now? Maybe the answer is to continue reading this book. And if that's true, let's connect in this moment through God, friend-to-friend style, with a prayer.

> Dear Lord, I always want to start off praising you. You give me so much and you fill me up. Until now, I didn't stop to ask why I deserved to have you breathe life into me. I didn't wonder why you gave me a brain that helps me do so many tasks I take for granted, like deciphering the symbols on this page, as I read and learn something new about you and myself. But now I'm stopping for a moment. I'm breathing deeply, enjoying each breath, and I hope you don't mind me saying this, but I think you've given me breath and kept me alive because the world needs me. Dear Lord, this world is waiting for my next contribution. That's why you gave me gifts. And because I am important, I'm going to ask that you allow me to get better at taking care of myself, at loving myself, better at keeping my heart open and filled with your love. Thank you, Jesus, and praise be your name. Amen.

How was that for you? Be sure to keep an ear out for the soothing quality of your internal maternal voice. If you were brought up in harsh circumstances, you may find that you speak to yourself with sarcasm, or even insults. You might look at something you've accomplished and think: "Oh, come on, you can do better than this?" Or you might think, "The world is waiting for your contribution, hah!" Or at some point, when you need to rouse your tired body, you might hear yourself thinking, "Get with it, girl."

There's a way to change the timbre of your internal voice. If you have a photo of yourself as a child or infant, pull it out. Make quiet time for yourself, lighting a few candles if possible. Sit comfortably and breathe deeply. Look at the picture and speak to yourself. Lee has a photo of herself as an infant, and although her beloved mother has passed away years earlier and she can't confirm her idea, Lee's convinced that this photo was taken when she was eight months old, a few days before her mother took her down south and left Lee and her sister with their grandparents.

"The smile on my face is so tentative," Lee says, "as if my mom was standing in the background at the photographer's studio, encouraging me to smile. I was wearing a pretty little cotton dress and the corners of my mouth are turned up, but my eyes look so unhappy, as if I sense that I'll be separated from my mom for a long time. I don't blame my mother for leaving me. She did what she had to. My father had deserted us and she needed to get a full-time job to support us. But pain is pain. If someone steps on your foot and breaks your toe, it may be an accident, but that doesn't mean your toe won't throb. That's what I feel when I look at the picture. I think about a hurt, abandoned girl."

Lee has learned to talk to the photo, and in this manner she has developed a strong and soothing internal voice. "I might say something like, 'Hello, you beautiful darling girl. I love you so much. You are so precious. I thank God for you. You don't have to smile if you don't want to. Let me just hold you and stroke your lovely head.' "

Sometimes that supportive voice can come from caring others. Not too long ago I received a beautifully framed photograph as a gift, and I was about to take it to my church, thinking my parishioners would enjoy it, when my assistant stopped me and said, "Pastor, you love that picture and you're always giving to others. Why not put it in your office?" She was right, and that's just what I did. I love looking up and seeing the photo and remembering her kind words. This is the tone you're striving for, one that's complimentary and supportive.

For some of us, developing an internal mothering voice will be close to rewriting our own history. And let me tell you, it can transform your life. Because when your heart softens, so will your demeanor. Your eyes, your skin, everything about you will reflect your self-regard. When we love ourselves, we become capable of visualizing ourselves with someone who holds us in high regard.

Maybe you've given up on romance. Perhaps you've told yourself that there are no good men around. Think about what you're really saying. If low self-regard had led you to become involved in relationships that were abusive or demeaning, no wonder you believed that. You may have looked at men who did care for you as boring losers. Do you get the connection? When you don't love yourself, you assume that anyone that does love you mustn't be worth much.

But a new day is dawning and you want to open yourself to new possibilities. Keep in mind that it is written in I John 4:8, "He that loveth not knoweth not God; for God is love." Don't limit yourself to a life without love because you're tied to old beliefs. Here's a new belief to replace the old one: God, who is love, wants you to have love.

And that's the gospel truth.

PART III

BLESSED ENERGY

CHAPTER 8

Revving Up Your Emotional Energy

I f you've read Parts I and II, for the letters *B* and *L* in "blessed," and you're wondering how you'll drum up motivation to follow through on suggested ideas and actions, you've turned to the right page. This chapter is designed to help you figure out what you'll need to do to generate more get-up-and-go.

Right off the bat, I can tell you that boosting your emotional energy level can make a major difference in the quality of your life and future achievements. With that said, you're probably wondering what I mean by emotional energy. Rather than explaining what that is or how to boost it, I encourage you to take the Emotional Energy Quotient (EEQ) Test, which I've designed for those who want to learn how to live like they're blessed. It will provide a reasonably accurate analysis of your motivational level and help you understand why you need high reserves of emotional energy.

You'll want to choose answers that best reflect your responses. If you reach a situation that doesn't apply to your life, think about what you would do. You will find three possible responses. If two or more answers seem to fit your response, choose the one closest to your situation. Try to answer spontaneously. No one is looking over your shoulder judging you. It would be a waste of your time and even misleading if you choose the answer you thought you should pick or that sounded "right." There is no right or wrong here. Your goal is to live like you're blessed.

You'll need a sheet of paper and pen or pencil to keep score. Fold the sheet lengthwise into fourths. In the far-left column write "Red" at the top; in the next column, "Yellow"; then "Blue" in the next; and in the final column, write "Green" at the top. Please put the paper aside for now and concentrate on responding to the situations in the EEQ.

The Emotional Energy Quotient Test

I. You wake up and wonder how you'll ever get everything done.
Ⓐ Never   Ⓑ Occasionally   Ⓒ Frequently

2. You feel angry.
Ⓐ Never   Ⓑ Occasionally   Ⓒ Frequently

3. You're in a physically or emotionally abusive relationship.
Ⓐ Never   Ⓑ Occasionally   Ⓒ Frequently

4. At day's end, you're satisfied with what you've accomplished.
Ⓐ Never   Ⓑ Occasionally   Ⓒ Frequently

5. Your dresser drawers and bedroom closets are neat.
Ⓐ Never   Ⓑ Occasionally   Ⓒ Frequently

6. You love swimming and often engage in this sport.

    Ⓐ Never   Ⓑ Occasionally   Ⓒ Frequently

7. When it comes to least-favorite tasks—such as filing taxes, filling out expense reports, or getting your teeth cleaned—you procrastinate until it's almost too late.

    Ⓐ Never   Ⓑ Occasionally   Ⓒ Frequently

8. You make time to see supportive friends and relatives.

    Ⓐ Never   Ⓑ Occasionally   Ⓒ Frequently

9. You attend church and tithe.

    Ⓐ Never   Ⓑ Occasionally   Ⓒ Frequently

10. You often express creativity through drawing, singing, writing, or other endeavors.

    Ⓐ Never   Ⓑ Occasionally   Ⓒ Frequently

11. You balance your checkbook.

    Ⓐ Never   Ⓑ Occasionally   Ⓒ Frequently

12. You remain in an unfulfilling job.

    Ⓐ Never   Ⓑ Occasionally   Ⓒ Frequently

13. You smoke, overeat, drink too much alcohol, or engage in another unhealthy addiction.

    Ⓐ Never   Ⓑ Occasionally   Ⓒ Frequently

14. You make New Year's resolutions that you keep.

    Ⓐ Never   Ⓑ Occasionally   Ⓒ Frequently

15. You want to give a party but you're too busy.

    Ⓐ Never   Ⓑ Occasionally   Ⓒ Frequently

16. When an individual says or does something that makes you uncomfortable, you speak up for yourself in an appropriate manner.

    Ⓐ Never   Ⓑ Occasionally   Ⓒ Frequently

17. You use the Internet.

    Ⓐ Never   Ⓑ Occasionally   Ⓒ Frequently

18. When you're not working, you're usually alone or on the phone.

    Ⓐ Never   Ⓑ Occasionally   Ⓒ Frequently

19. You exercise regularly.

    Ⓐ Never   Ⓑ Occasionally   Ⓒ Frequently

20. You pray regularly.

    Ⓐ Never   Ⓑ Occasionally   Ⓒ Frequently

21. You worry about someone you care about.

    Ⓐ Never   Ⓑ Occasionally   Ⓒ Frequently

22. You get sick with colds, the flu, or other infections.

    Ⓐ Never   Ⓑ Occasionally   Ⓒ Frequently

23. You get a good night's sleep.

    Ⓐ Never   Ⓑ Occasionally   Ⓒ Frequently

24. You have someone in your life with whom you share affection.

    Ⓐ Never   Ⓑ Occasionally   Ⓒ Frequently

25. You perform volunteer work.

    Ⓐ Never   Ⓑ Occasionally   Ⓒ Frequently

Now pull out that sheet of paper with the four columns. Every response below is followed by a color: red, yellow, blue, or green. If your response to situation 1 corresponds with red, write the number 1 in the red column. If your response to situation 2 corresponds with green, write the number 2 in the green column, and so on. When you finish, you'll have twenty-five different numbers dispersed among the four columns.

Responses to Situation 1

A. If you awake and *never* wonder how you'll get everything done, you're laid back to the point of being blasé or you may not feel sufficiently challenged. If that's so, you'll want to look for meaningful opportunities to use your many God-given talents. You'll also want to consider whether this lack of concern is an indication that life's trials have robbed you of passion. **Green**

B. If you *occasionally* wonder how you'll get everything done, you may have a fairly balanced schedule. Unforeseen

events do interrupt plans, and if we live creative and
dynamic lives we're able to roll with the punches. **Green**

C. If you *frequently* wonder how you'll get everything done,
you're overextended and this is a major energy drain. I
feel this way at times, and often say that I don't just have
a lot on my plate, I have a lot on my platter. Moving
from restful sleep to instant alert is hard on your body. If
you're doing too much for others, insist that they help. As
you find ways to pare down your schedule, use your
nurturing inner voice to remind yourself that you deserve
to make time for your own needs. You are important to
God. **Yellow**

Put a 1 in the appropriate column.

Responses to Situation 2

A. If you imagine that you *never* feel angry, you may be
in denial about this very natural response. If you think
it's un-Christian to get angry, remember Jesus cleansing
the temple of the money changers (John 2:15). He
was righteously angry about God's values being
violated. He lost his temper because he was human.
Everybody has some anger, and if you're denying and
suppressing it, you're experiencing a serious energy drain.
Yellow

B. If you *occasionally* feel angry, you may be good at reading
your own emotions. Remember, this question is about
how you feel, not how you behave. Seething after your
supervisor scolds you is a natural response. Blowing up at
him might get you fired, but a healthy alternative might

be lunching with a supportive coworker and letting off steam. Like real steam, anger can build up, and when it comes to bodies, this emotional pressure can create health problems. If you're aware of times when you're angry and find healthy ways to express it, you're conserving emotional energy. **Green**

C. If you're *frequently* angry, good for you for recognizing that. That kind of anger often stems from long-term issues, and you may want to use your journal to explore unresolved pain from hurtful childhood experiences. Anger doesn't simply go away, it remains in your body and can affect your energy level and damage your health. **Red**

Put a 2 in the appropriate column.

Responses to Situation 3

A. If you would *never* remain in an abusive relationship, you know how to treat yourself lovingly. **Green**

B. If you're *occasionally* abused by a partner, you may be convinced that you're staying in the relationship to keep up appearances or for the sake of your children. Couldn't that just be an excuse? Children are never a good reason for staying in a hurtful relationship. Children or no children, if you're being treated in an inhumane fashion, you are getting by on the dregs of your emotional energy reserve. **Red**

C. If you're *frequently* abused, you may have grown up in a home in which you witnessed violence between your parents or you may have been abused. If you are in an abusive relationship, I urge you not to wait until it's too late to leave. God gave us a sense of pain as a sudden and startling way of reminding ourselves what we should avoid, and that includes avoiding people who hurt us. You probably feel terrified, and fear can deplete your emotional energy. **Red**

Put a 3 in the appropriate column.

Responses to Situation 4

A. If you *never* feel satisfied with what you've accomplished, you may be overscheduled or might be holding yourself to impossible standards. **Yellow**

B. If you *occasionally* feel satisfied with what you've accomplished, you'll want to look closer at your life. Try writing in your journal to consider what you can do to better appreciate your contributions, and follow your own good advice. **Blue**

C. If you *frequently* feel satisfied with what you've accomplished, then you view your contributions as worthwhile. You place great value in your day-to-day endeavors, and your emotional energy level may be helping you maintain a balanced schedule. **Green**

Put a 4 in the appropriate column.

Responses to Situation 5

A. If your dresser drawers and bedroom closets are *never* neat, you probably aren't making time to care for yourself. This is not about the quality of your housekeeping.

Dresser drawers and bedroom closets are repositories for
your personal items. On busy days, if they're messy, you'll
be left scrambling. **Yellow**

B. If your dresser drawers and closets are *occasionally* neat, it
sounds like you sometimes take the time to straighten
them up. Even if your life isn't as balanced as you'd like,
you sense the need to take care of yourself. **Blue**

C. If your dresser drawers and closets are *frequently* neat, that
doesn't mean you're a housekeeping perfectionist. Dressers
and bedroom closets are the repositories of items that
help you make your way through the world. While they
may not reflect the most fashionable or expensive of
tastes, they enhance your sense of self. **Green**

Put a 5 in the appropriate column.

Responses to Situation 6

A. If you *never* swim because you hate getting your hair
wet, keep in mind that people with balanced lives are
flexible and open to experiencing the world. Maintaining
a hairstyle with every strand in place doesn't allow for
spontaneity. And if it is fear that is keeping you from
taking the plunge, consider taking a class for the water-
shy. My mom learned to swim as an adult, after she
realized that my brother and I, who had become avid
swimmers, were going to spend a lot of time in pools.
Like so many others before her, she found that
swimming reduces stress and offers a low-impact aerobic
workout. And consider this: Two-thirds of God's earth is

covered in water. Swimming imparts a sense of physical mastery over the world, while fear zaps emotional energy. **Yellow**

B. If you *occasionally* swim, that means you've learned how and you understand the pleasures of moving through the water. If keeping your do in place is keeping you from taking the plunge more often, try scheduling swims before the beauty salon. Swimming implies certain flexibility in one's lifestyle. Good for you. **Blue**

C. If you *frequently* swim you've learned to feel at one with the earth. I've just started swimming three to four times a week, early mornings, and I love it. After all, humans come to life and are sustained in the fluids in our mothers' wombs, so it should not be surprising that swimming has a calming effect. **Green**

Put a 6 in the appropriate column.

Responses to Situation 7

A. If you *never* put off least-favorite tasks until the last minute you are in a rarefied minority, and I can only take my cap off to you. It sounds as if you've fashioned a well-honed schedule. With the less pleasurable aspects out of the way, you've made time for fun and spontaneity. **Green**

B. If you *occasionally* put off least-favorite tasks until the last minute you're likely to run into me on the waiting line, and we'll have plenty of company. Life is rushed and busy and although we're working at making it run like a well-oiled machine, we haven't gotten there yet. **Blue**

C. If you *frequently* put off least-favorite tasks you may often feel out of control and nervous. Anxiety is right up there at the top of the list for energy drains. **Yellow**

Put a 7 in the appropriate column.

Responses to Situation 8

A. If you *never* make time to see supportive family and friends, you're socially isolating yourself, and that's punishing. Supportive family and friends are a blessing. Just recently, my Aunt Bertha, who was one of my mother's best friends and godmother to my sons, advised me about what to wear for my annual sermon as president of the Hampton Ministers' Conference. When Aunt Bertha deemed a suit "just right," "too matronly," or "in need of tapering," I appreciated every word. We all deserve the sense of relaxation that is imparted when we spend time with friends. Supportive family is an additional plus because they're the ones who keep us in touch with where we came from. They are truly our roots and keep us grounded. **Yellow**

B. If you *occasionally* make time to see family and friends, you're headed in the right direction. Since these individuals can sustain you during hard times, you'll want to boost those connections by figuring out how you can see them more often. **Blue**

C. If you *frequently* make time to see family and friends, you feel their blessing. They let you vent when you need to, give you sound advice when you need it, and offer opportunities to exchange hugs and deep belly laughs. They boost your energy level. **Green**

Put an 8 in the appropriate column.

Responses to Situation 9

A. If you *never* attend church or tithe, that's akin to pulling the plug out of your radio and wondering why you can't hear the music. You'll know you've found the right church if you return home feeling as if your batteries have been recharged. I'm not saying this because I'm a minister. Just praising Jesus makes me feel energized. Hallelujah and get thee to the church, sista! **Yellow**

B. If you *occasionally* attend church and tithe, you already understand why you need to, but you haven't fully committed yourself to the Lord. If you find the right services, you won't use being tired as an excuse not to attend; you'll want to attend so you won't feel tired anymore. **Blue**

C. If you *frequently* attend church and tithe you may have found one that gives you back as much as you give, and you know that's a blessing. With the right spiritual boost, you'll find that all during the week when you encounter difficulties, you can keep on keeping on. **Green**

Put a 9 in the appropriate column.

Responses to Situation 10

A. If you *never* express your creativity, your highest self is trapped within you. Since we're made in God's image, we're filled with the power of creativity. One woman,

Yvonne, used to complain that she had no creative talent, but after praying on it she began designing gift baskets of flowers and baked goods that she delivered to the sick and shut-ins. Ask God to help you develop your creativity, and then after listing what you enjoy doing, your gifts will be revealed. **Yellow**

B. If you *occasionally* express your creativity, ask yourself what you can do to make this a more dominant aspect of your life. The world is waiting for you. **Blue**

C. If you *frequently* express your creativity, you may be earning your living by utilizing one of your talents. If so, rev up your engine by tapping into another outlet for your creativity. If you don't earn your living with a creative talent, consider how you might and go for it. **Green**

Put a 10 in the appropriate column.

Responses to Situation 11

A. If you *never* balance your checkbook, face it, you've given control of your money to a bank clerk who may make mistakes—but always in the bank's favor. Few people enjoy setting aside time to balance a checkbook, but those who master the discipline are people who take care of their finances. You deserve to have all the money you earn, while those who live in a state of financial chaos have unbalanced statements and unbalanced lives. **Yellow**

B. You *occasionally* balance your checkbook, which means you know it's a good habit to develop. Some people follow a can't balance; can't spend rule. What that means is that once a month, after payday, they don't allow themselves to spend any money on anything pleasurable—ice cream, videos, dinner out—until the checkbook is balanced. Try that. **Blue**

C. If you *frequently* balance your checkbook you're developing the kind of habits that will lead you to financial abundance, which sure makes it easier to sleep deeply. **Green**

Put an 11 in the appropriate column.

Responses to Situation 12

A. You *never* stay in an unfulfilling job? If that means you skip from job to job, try hanging in there a bit longer and giving yourself time to rise to the challenge. That will help you develop a discipline that will aid you in your next endeavor. But if it means you'd never stay in a dead-end job without marshalling your efforts to find something better, then you're prepared to fight for the quality of your life. Congratulations. The effort alone will add to your emotional energy score. **Green**

B. If you *occasionally* remain in unfulfilling jobs, you're doing what you can to keep the money flowing, and hats off to you. You will also want to work at shutting down any ill will you may feel once you're in the workplace, or you'll wind up hurting yourself by getting fired. In the meantime, cultivate new skills so you can move on to something better. **Blue**

C. If you *frequently* remain in unfulfilling jobs, then take a look at your work history and ask yourself what you've learned from each one. That's right, even that 7-Eleven convenience store job, where the owner's agitated Doberman watched your every move, offered a lesson. Maybe you learned a particular life lesson. Now, here's the next question: What can you do with all those lessons so you can find more fulfilling work? **Yellow**

Put a 12 in the appropriate column.

Responses to Situation 13

A. If you *never* smoke, overeat, drink too much alcohol or engage in any behavior harmful to your health, you treat your body as the temple that it is. And you're probably looking and feeling pretty good, which is its own reward. **Green**

B. If you *occasionally* smoke, overeat, drink too much, or engage in any harmful behavior, you act like the majority of the people in the world. But remember that *trying* isn't good enough. Overdoing any behavior is a sign that your life is out of balance. **Blue**

C. If you *frequently* smoke, overeat, drink too much alcohol, or overdo anything else harmful to your health, this is addictive behavior. It may have already ~erfered with your intimate relationships. Compulsive behavior is a defense for childhood experiences in which people were made to feel shame. Your emotional energy reserve is almost on empty. But the news isn't all bad; be assured that there's a professional out there waiting for you to call, wanting to serve God by helping you heal. Please make that call. **Red**

Put a 13 in the appropriate column.

Responses to Situation 14

A. You make New Year's resolutions that you *never* keep. My response to that one is a big "So what?" Making New Year's resolutions is a game. While the tradition may boost profits at health clubs, after people who want to start exercising regularly sign up and then stop attending a month later, there's no stipulation that says you're supposed to feel guilty about not following them. Make a list of some of the resolutions you've never followed and use it as a reminder of what you really want to change in your life and then take it to the Lord in prayer. Now that's a resolution you'll want to keep. While you're at it, thank God for your sense of humor, because smiling and laughing can certainly boost your emotional energy reserve. **Blue**

B. If you *occasionally* keep New Year's Resolutions, you have benefited from this game—and it *is* a game. But if you're better off as a result of keeping those resolutions, who would complain? Make a list of the resolutions you've adhered to and pat yourself on the back. As for those you haven't followed, ask God for help in changing. You're more likely to stick to the plan when prayer is involved. **Blue**

C. If you *frequently* keep New Year's Resolutions, you really view this first-of-the-year game as a promise that you've made to yourself. That's admirable, and it's also a sign that your emotional energy is helping you function at a high level. Be sure to thank God for your discipline. **Green**

Put a 14 in the appropriate column.

Responses to Situation 15

A. If you *never* have time to give parties, you may be using a busy schedule as an excuse for not celebrating your life. Even busy people make time for parties. Parties allow us to make our houses homes. When the event is in full swing, you'll see people who care about you coming together, enjoying one another and you. Parties help us feel restored and renewed. **Yellow**

B. If you *occasionally* give parties, then you know how to enjoy your friends and good times. Parties require emotional and physical energy: sending out the invitations, preparing the food, and cleaning the house. There's usually anxiety leading up to the event, but boy, will you experience a natural high once things are in full swing. **Green**

C. If you *frequently* give parties, you either have paid staff (aren't you fortunate—and I hope you're treating them with respect) or you're extremely spontaneous. Spontaneity certainly signifies a life well lived. **Green**

Put a 15 in the appropriate column.

Responses to Situation 16

A. If you *never* speak up when people do or say something that makes you uncomfortable, frustration may be tamping down your emotional energy. One woman couldn't bring herself to scold the maintenance man who always rubbed her back when she passed him in the hallway of her apartment building. She was annoyed with herself for not speaking up sooner, especially after he used the building key to enter her apartment—without ringing! At that point she told him off. Her outburst, and the energy it wasted, could have been avoided if she'd reminded him early on that some boundaries should never be crossed. **Yellow**

B. If you *occasionally* speak up when people do or say something that makes you uncomfortable, that's a start, but it's not enough when it comes to your well-being. People struggling with this issue have to practice speaking up. They have the disease to please, and they haven't developed their own emotional voices. The next time you run into an uncomfortable situation, think of a way of expressing yourself that will leave you with your dignity intact. If this proves to be difficult for you, learn to use a blanket statement. You might say, "That's not okay with me." **Blue**

C. If you *frequently* speak up in an appropriate manner (which means not "going off" on the person) when people say or do something that makes you uncomfortable, you've learned to care for yourself. If you feel an embarrassed flush after speaking up, use your internal nurturing voice and assure yourself that you've done what was necessary. **Green**

Put a 16 in the appropriate column.

Responses to Situation 17

A. If you *never* use the Internet you're cutting yourself off from a world filled with information. Sure there's some inappropriate stuff to be found online, but the technology is now so advanced that most of the uglier aspects of the Internet can be blocked from view. If you're not using the Internet and insist on communicating with everyone through snail mail, you're wasting time and energy that could be better spent, and you're giving into fears that lead you to believe it's too difficult for you to learn. I understand that kind of hesitancy. After decades of typing on a manual Royal typewriter I had to talk myself into taking that big step, and started signing up for computer classes during our family cruises. I couldn't even pretend I was too old to learn. My mother learned at seventy, so she could keep apprised of operations in the security company she owned and supervised. If you can't afford a computer, use one at the library and get a free e-mail address. **Yellow**

B. If you *occasionally* use the Internet then you've learned to use a tool that will only continue to be expanded upon. Now's the time to take that next step and get comfortable enough to navigate the Web. You can click into everything from biblical verses, to information on how to find favorite recipes, to finding whatever item you're searching for in your neighborhood. It brings the world in close, and by utilizing this time saver you'll have energy left over for good works. **Green**

C. If you *frequently* use the Internet, this may imply a fearlessness that helps you navigate through the world. **Green**

Put a 17 in the appropriate column.

Responses to Situation 18

A. If you're *never* alone during nonworking hours, you may be longing for solitude. Time alone offers opportunities for regrouping and introspection, and it suggests that you enjoy your own company. But if you're never alone because you can't stand solitude, there may be aspects of your life that you're afraid of confronting. If that's the case, journaling is the perfect opportunity for you to be with yourself and explore any uneasiness you feel about being solo. **Yellow**

B. If you're *occasionally* alone, explore through journal writing whether you prefer your own company or spending time with others. If you prefer being alone, you may have grown up hearing a parent or significant adult express similar feelings. How would you describe that individual's emotional life? Was it one that you'd like to emulate? Also write about how you felt if that individual didn't want to spend time with you. If you aren't usually alone, these periods of solitude will offer opportunities for replenishing your emotional energy. **Green**

C. If you are *frequently* alone you may have cut yourself off from vital connections. You may argue that you're alone by choice, but the question is why do you choose an isolated life? That's a topic to explore in your journal. **Yellow**

Put an 18 in the appropriate column.

Responses to Situation 19

A. If you *never* exercise, you're doing your body a great disservice. Regular exercise promotes good health, and it will certainly boost your emotional energy level. **Yellow**

B. If you *occasionally* exercise you're getting on the good foot, but try to talk yourself beyond this halfway commitment. The best way to exercise regularly is to ask a friend or colleague to join you. You can keep one another motivated. **Blue**

C. If you *frequently* exercise, folks have probably commented on how good you're looking, and that can only make you feel better. Regular exercise is energizing. **Green**

Put a 19 in the appropriate column.

Responses to Situation 20

A. If you've *never* developed the discipline of regular prayer, then ask yourself why. God is waiting for you to communicate through prayer. Go ahead, stop reading and speak to the Almighty. You'll be all the better for it. **Yellow**

B. If you *occasionally* pray, there's nothing to stop you from establishing a more permanent connection. As a matter of fact, there's no better time than right now. **Blue**

C. If you *frequently* pray, unlike the guy in the commercial, you don't have to ask: "Can you hear me now?" You know God is listening. When it comes to loving God and filling your emotional energy reservoir, there's no such thing as too much prayer. **Green**

Put a 20 in the appropriate column.

Responses to Situation 21

A. If you *never* worry about someone you care about, you are absolutely awesome. You've reached a point of nirvana. Worrying is an emotional energy drain. **Green**

B. If you *occasionally* worry about someone you love you have developed a close working relationship with the Almighty. Lee tells the story of how, two hours after walking her son to the school bus stop, she received a phone call from his headmaster asking why the boy wasn't in school. She asked the headmaster to call back as soon as he had any news, and immediately bent her head in prayer: "Lord, please hold me in your arms while I wait to hear good news." The phone rang minutes later and the headmaster apologized over an attendance error. Her son was in class. She thanked him for calling and then she turned back to the Lord and thanked him for soothing her anxieties. **Green**

C. If you *frequently* worry about someone you love, enlist your friends and family members as prayer warriors. Write them (hopefully via e-mail), tell them your concerns, and ask them to pray with you for a positive outcome. Worry feels like acid eating away at your stomach lining and will surely deplete your emotional energy. **Yellow**

Put a 21 in the appropriate column.

Responses to Situation 22

A. If you *never* come down with colds, viral infections, or the flu, your efforts to create balance in your life are paying off. Researchers have established a direct connection between a low immune system and high levels of stress and anxiety. **Green**

B. If you *occasionally* get colds, viral infections or the flu, your immune system seems to be functioning well. According to researchers, our immune systems work best when we work through anger, stress, and anxiety, rather than trying to suppress these emotions. **Green**

C. If you *frequently* get colds, viral infections or the flu, read *You Can Heal Your Life* by Louise L. Hay or *Emotional Intelligence* by Daniel Goleman, so you understand how you can improve your health by clearing away emotional energy blocks. Frequent ailments can leave you feeling drained. **Yellow**

Put a 22 in the appropriate column.

Responses to Situation 23

A. If you *never* get a good night's sleep I urge you to advocate on your own behalf. Sleep is absolutely necessary for boosting your emotional energy. Sleep-deprived people are less likely to exercise, they become depressed and irritable, and their responses are slowed. Sleep deficits can put you at a higher risk for accidents, and you're more likely to put on extra, unwanted weight. Consult your doctor and if necessary try alternative holistic approaches. **Yellow**

B. If you *occasionally* get a good night's sleep, you're settling for less than you require for good health. After three or four weeks of sleep loss, a weakened immune system will make you more susceptible to colds, flu, and other infectious diseases. Sleep helps us rebuild energy, so find a way to make it happen. **Blue**

C. If you *frequently* get a good night's sleep, you awake feeling refreshed and restored. This is one of the best gifts you can give your body and it will put you in the mood to get up and get going. Since I need eight hours of sleep, most people know not to call me after 9:30 p.m., except for emergencies. You too might want to pass the word around about your sleep needs. **Green**

Put a 23 in the appropriate column.

Responses to Situation 24

A. If you *never* receive and give affection you may be feeling the loss. Affection is rejuvenating. I'm reminded of this when I conduct "Wonderful Wall Street Wednesdays," at St. John United Methodist Church, in Manhattan's financial district, from Memorial Day through Labor Day. People of various Christian denominations, races and ethnicities walk in looking burdened by the tensions of the stock market. After they turn to one another (at my suggestion) and offer each other hugs and encouragement, their faces glow and they leave smiling. **Yellow**

B. If you *occasionally* receive and give affection, you remember how good it feels. After World War II, doctors visiting European orphanages found that some babies had stopped growing. The infants had been fed and clothed, but because the orphanages were understaffed, the children had not received affection. Doctors call this syndrome "failure to thrive." From the day we're born until the day we die, we need love and affection. **Blue**

C. If you *frequently* receive and give affection, you're taking it in, allowing it to fill you up. God gave us sensitive skin and fingertips because we were meant to touch loved ones, so enjoy. **Green**

Put a 24 in the appropriate column.

Responses to Situation 25

A. If you *never* engage in volunteer work, you're suggesting by your inaction that you're too tired or too busy to serve as God's hands. You don't have to sign up at an organization. Lee made it a point to greet strangers at the cooperative apartment complex where she lives. She baked items to welcome newcomers and introduced them to other neighbors. One of these people turned out to be a wealthy woman who put up a substantial sum of money so Lee and her family could move to a larger apartment. Lee didn't greet strangers to get something back, but that's the nature of doing for others. You put that energy out into the world and one way or another it comes back and enriches your life. **Yellow**

B. If you *occasionally* engage in volunteer work you know the enriching experience of serving as God's hands. If you can't schedule time to perform a regular service, ask God to show you how you can make more of an impact with your time and your gifts. **Green**

C. If you *frequently* engage in volunteer work you serve as a force for good and this replenishes your emotional energy reserve. You allow your contributions to take your mind off your own problems. And your efforts make you grateful for all that you have. **Green**

Put a 25 in the appropriate column.

Now you can tally your score. Twenty-eight different figures are dispersed throughout the color columns. Tally up the numbers in each column. For instance, you may have two numbers in the red column, nine in the yellow, eight in blue, and six in green. Figure out which column has the most numbers, which column has the second highest number of figures, which comes in third, and which last.

Here's how to read your emotional energy level. Red is the column for emotional baggage. By that, I mean the issues that may stem from childhood and that are weighing you down, like toxic shame and long-term anger. If you have any numbers in the red column, you are more likely to feel dragged down. If you are high functioning despite all this baggage, you may still feel emotionally drained.

If you scored high in the yellow level, your emotional energy reserve is medium-low. It's like having the gas gauge on your car slightly above the empty mark. You know that if you don't fill up soon you'll likely run out of gas and wind up in trouble. If you have most of your scores in the red and yellow area, you are running on fumes.

A high score in the blue range indicates a medium-to-high emotional energy range. You're close to creating the balanced life you desire.

And last, but definitely not least in the scoring is the green range. Green represents spring, when Jesus rose from the dead, and it symbolizes new life. If most of your scores divided between the blue and green areas, you have a high emotional reserve. No matter what your score, you'll want to note thoughts and feelings that came to you. By working through this Emotional Energy Test, you know which areas of your life need a boost.

Finally, here's a color coding system that might help you in your scheduling. I use colored markers to help me keep my schedule balanced. In my calendar, I fill in out-of-town trips in yellow; pink means I'm making a speech; blue days are for times when I've scheduled rest periods; and green indicates family time. As I look over my schedule, I keep an eye out for blue (rest) dates, and if I don't have enough, that is a sign that my schedule is out of balance. If I see too many yellow (out-of-town) days, I know to cut back on upcoming engagements. And no matter how important an engagement may sound, I never budge if I have an invitation for a blue (family) day. Using this system, I was able to attend my son Samuel's middle school basketball games (the team made it to the championships!).

It took me awhile to learn to use this system efficiently, but it seems everyone in our family has caught on. When Ron and I were young parents and had overscheduled our sons' weekend, Christopher, who was five at the time, said, "Next Saturday I want to stay home, get up late, watch television, and have a Me day." It was a great idea. All of us could use a few Me days to keep ourselves from feeling drained. In the next chapter you'll meet a woman who was running on empty and was confronted with religious issues that might have kept her from creating the balance she needed in her life.

CHAPTER 9

Healing Depression

As we continue to explore the *E* for emotional energy in "blessed," this is a good time to introduce the vivacious and pretty Marilyn, who was usually the life of the party. Quick to smile and with a luminous intelligence apparent in her big brown eyes, she has a gift for getting the most uptight sort of folks to relax. Her charisma is a real plus in her work as an investigative reporter on TV. On one morning that she recalled, her smile seemed washed away by her tears, and the emotional energy that had kept her going for forty-three years seemed to have dissolved from her body. "I was shattered. I kept telling myself to get out of bed, but I kept laying there."

Marilyn reminded herself that women in her family didn't act like this. But the pride that was usually generated when she thought of the strong, independent black women that had come before her wasn't doing the trick that day. "I couldn't understand why it had affected me so deeply."

The "it" she referred to was the breakup of her second marriage. After a year together, her husband had moved out on the first day of December, and eleven days later, the divorce papers arrived. Reading the words that signaled an official end to their union probably shouldn't have been such a surprise. After all, she and Benjamin had certainly engaged in their share of disagreements, especially when it came to his teenage daughter, who along with Benjamin, had moved into Marilyn's comfortable Detroit home.

"His daughter was seventeen and completely out of control, staying out all night, but he wouldn't say anything to her. And he got angry with me when I caught her in a lie. I think he felt guilty because her mom was a heavy drinker, so this girl hadn't had a great mother. He was trying to make it up to her."

Despite the couple's differences, Marilyn had expected that she and Benjamin would work them out, especially through prayer. After all, their mutual faith was what brought them together in the first place. Benjamin was an assistant minister at her Baptist church, and as someone who was "new to the Lord" Marilyn found his biblical interpretations spellbinding. "He was a biblical scholar. I thought he could really teach me something, and he also fit my quote-unquote checklist. He was handsome, and intelligent, and before working for the church he'd earned a law degree and served as a judge. On top of all that, he was divorced and raising a daughter. I found the whole package appealing."

Benjamin seemed to admire her too and gave her every impression of being deeply in love with her. As a new arrival to Detroit, Benjamin had put on a full-court press as he pursued Marilyn. "He swept me off my feet: brought me flowers at work. And once when I went out of town, he showed up at the airport wearing a tuxedo to celebrate my return. I pictured us settling down together and studying the Bible."

But that was not to be. One morning Benjamin announced that he was leaving her—that day. "It was the beginning of the Christmas season, and a few weeks later, when one of my friends dropped by, he said he'd just seen Benjamin and his daughter at another woman's house. They'd moved in with her and they were decorating a tree."

Four days after being served with the divorce papers, Marilyn dragged herself to the office. "My boss took one look at me and said, 'You're falling apart. You can't work like this.' I thought, 'Oh God, I'm going to lose my job.' "

She didn't need a specialist to know she was depressed. Everyone gets the blues now and then, she told herself, and besides, her grief was normal. She'd have worried about herself if she hadn't felt depressed. She resumed her work schedule, but as she continued dragging through her days, feeling weak and disinterested in life, she knew that she was suffering from something a lot bigger than disappointment.

In fact Marilyn was clinically depressed. According to Dr. Brenda Wade, coauthor with Brenda Lane Richardson of *What Mama Couldn't Tell Us About Love*, symptoms of depression include, "hopelessness, fatigue, loss of interest in sex and other normally enjoyable activities." Also, according to Dr. Wade, depressed people tend to think pessimistically and are highly critical of others and themselves. Additionally, they may feel lethargic, cry frequently, over- or undereat, oversleep or suffer from insomnia, and mask symptoms with irritability and excessive worry. With all those negatives, depression could easily be called the major emotional energy drain.

As you learn the details of Marilyn's story, you'll discover the events that led up to her depressive episode. Her husband walking out on her was far from her first loss, but that did put her in touch with the abandonment she experienced in childhood. Like many successful people, Marilyn employed a combination of grit, determination, and talent to fight her way to the top, while trying to convince herself that she could ignore hurtful memories. But as we learned in the last chapter, emotions are energy. In fact, they are energy in motion. To function at our best, our energy needs to flow and move. Emotional baggage from childhood presses our energy down. That's what depression means, pressed down energy.

Also like many of us, one of Marilyn's greatest blessings was her faith in God. And throughout her ordeal, her relationship with God remained firmly intact. For some people their faith collides with the question of how to deal with depression or other emotional maladies, which they feel they should be able to "snap out of." Maybe you or someone you know questions whether these maladies can be dealt with through reliance on God. Some people point to the biblical story of Paul pleading for a cure from his pain, when God told him in (2 Corinthians 12:9), "My grace is sufficient for you, for my strength is made perfect in weakness."

What a blessed gift. By the grace of God, He promises to be with us even in adversity. He urges us to use our struggles as an opportunity to increase our faith. A lot of us make the mistake of judging God's love through providence. What I mean by that is that when our lives are going well—maybe we got the raise we'd hoped for or a relationship is progressing smoothly—we might think, God really loves me. And we would be right, He does. But He loves us just as much when we're experiencing hardship. The test for us is whether we can love him just as much in our pain as in our happiness.

During those days in bed without food, Marilyn, like Paul, was fasting and praying, asking God to make it better. What do you think she should have done to relieve her symptoms? Did her lack of improvement suggest that God wanted her to remain in pain? Should she have allowed her supervisor to become more concerned about her condition, perhaps even fire her?

I can tell you that Marilyn has a good life today, and rather than launching into an explanation about how that occurred, it's important for you to know the events that predated the collapse of her second marriage.

Marilyn was born in a rundown section of Portland, Oregon, not in a bed of roses. "My mother was a teenager when she got pregnant with me. She'd been living with her mom, who was divorced, and she'd never really known her dad. She was just about to finish high school, and really smart. Her dream was to escape from home and the life she had there."

But pregnancy put an end to her mother's dreams. "My mother viewed me as the one who tied her down. She had to get a job to support me."

For the first eight years of her life, Marilyn remained happily ensconced in the home of her maternal grandmother, who was fun-loving and generous. "I have memories of her bundling me up on chilly days and taking me out to play." Marilyn's mother would visit occasionally, and she also has vague memories of her father, who was forced by his parents to marry Marilyn's mother. "I remember him and my mother taking me to a pool. He carried me on his shoulders, and I was just above the water, kicking and playing. My mother was calling from the edge of the pool, telling him to bring me back to her. It's one of my fondest childhood memories."

When her parents divorced, Marilyn's mother remarried, and one day, her mother stopped by accompanied by the new stepfather. "That was the first time I met him. He was big, six-foot-nine, and he earned a good living as a contractor's assistant." Through the years, they had five children together. "My mother didn't have a lot of patience. My sister once told me a story about a time after I left home when Mom got really angry and locked all the rest of the kids in the garage. She told them, 'I never wanted to have children. I don't want you and I didn't want you.'" Marilyn once asked her mother why she'd had so many kids, and her mother told her that her husband wanted a large family. "She didn't stop having kids until birth control came out. My sisters and brothers are like stair steps. The only gap is when Mom had a backroom abortion."

During the younger years when Marilyn lived with her grandmother, she saw her mother during occasional visits, and learned quickly not to ask about her biological father. "She didn't like him, and she'd remind me that he never sent any money for my support, to put clothes on my back or food in my stomach."

When her beloved grandmother died, Marilyn went to live with her mother, and she praises her attributes. "My mother is a voracious reader, so we always had newspapers and magazines around the house. And she watched the news every night. She was an information addict, and that's certainly what led to my love of news. We were also one of the only families on the block to have a set of encyclopedias. People would come to our house when they wanted to look something up."

In her new home, living with her mother, there was a great deal expected of Marilyn, and she was eager to please. "It was my responsibility to keep an eye on the other children. My mother worked evenings at the post office, and she trusted me to keep meals on the table, and I did the laundry."

Although young, she wasn't overwhelmed by her responsibilities; young Marilyn saw it as a matter of being trusted rather than burdened. "The brother closest to me is five years younger and the next one is ten years younger, so I had to be a responsible adult from a young age. I was entrusted to teach them their alphabets, names, phone number, and address before they started school. My sister actually went the wrong way once, and based on what she'd learned, she rang a neighborhood bell, said she was lost, and gave her name, address, and phone number."

One privilege of being the oldest sibling was getting her own bedroom. Marilyn was ten when her stepfather first started coming in at night, while her mother was at work. "He was huge and I was a toothpick. I had no experience of dealing with men, and he was the father of my sisters and brothers. But he threatened to kill me if I told anyone. I didn't even feel like telling my mother. She loved him, and I was afraid of him. All of us were terrified of him. He could get loud and he spanked us and would get very dramatic, rolling the belt around his fist. My whole goal was not to get hurt, and to keep my siblings from getting hurt. Sometimes, if I knew that one of them might get beaten, I'd lie and take the blame and get beaten in their place. . . . So I didn't fight my stepfather when he forced himself on me. It wasn't until I was in my twenties that my sister told me he'd molested her too. She was damaged by it. She ran away and had drug issues."

Marilyn connects her own survival to God's grace, which included spending her first eight years with her loving grandmother. Marilyn also excelled at school, earning high grades and praise from her mother, whom she deeply loved and wanted to impress. "I was the hero in the family, the academic achiever. My mother told me I would never be pretty and that she wanted me to focus on getting good grades."

Meanwhile, her stepfather's sexual abuse continued for six years. "I'm convinced that my mother must have known, but she wasn't willing to give up her middle-class lifestyle for me." Marilyn told a classmate about her troubles, and the police were notified. Without warning, uniformed officers showed up at her predominantly white school and took Marilyn out, as if she were under arrest.

"They'd called my mother about the abuse, and she told them I was lying. She claimed I made it all up because my stepfather refused to let me date and that she would not keep a liar in her house. Back then the police didn't know how to deal with a situation like this." The officers took Marilyn to juvenile hall, where she remained for months. "My mother came to visit me once. She said I would have to stay until I told the authorities I was lying. I refused to take back what I'd said."

With her mother refusing to allow her to come home, Marilyn was sent to foster care, where she was again sexually abused. She was removed from that home, sent to another, and was again abused.

Feeling unloved and abandoned, Marilyn was drawn to the first man who complimented her. "I was sixteen, and fell for the oldest line in the book: 'Hey baby, you sure are fine.' Nobody had ever said that to me before. . . . Percy's full-time job was hanging outside the high school. He asked me for my phone number and said he wanted me to be his girlfriend. When I learned that he played a saxophone I was in love—musical talent, in addition to saying I was fine! I had sex with him. And wouldn't you know? One time and I was pregnant."

It was 1968, a time of social upheaval, but the circumstances were similar to when her mother had become pregnant at almost the same age: both of them smart women, lacking in self-love, tied to men who didn't want them.

"Percy's mother and grandmother insisted that he marry me," Marilyn says. "At first, we lived on welfare, but when my son was two years old I aced a test for a county job and they hired me." Arguments between the young couple often ended with Percy beating Marilyn. His grandmother convinced them that the baby would be better off living with her. Marilyn was too weary to argue otherwise and allowed the grandmother to take the baby. The situation was eerily reminiscent of what had occurred with Marilyn's own mother. When people carry around unhealed scars they often repeat their own parents' damaging patterns.

With no full-time child-rearing responsibilities, Marilyn took a friend's advice and enrolled in junior college. A few months later, when her husband blackened her eye and chipped her tooth, she decided to leave him, despite the fact that she was six months pregnant with their second child. This time Marilyn gave birth to a daughter. Struggling to work full time and attend college, she allowed Percy's grandmother to take this child too—the situation was supposed to be temporary.

Through the next few years, she spent time with her children on weekends and during vacations, and continued excelling at school. "One of my teachers at community college convinced me to apply for a scholarship to a four-year school." She was able to attend the University of Michigan, all expenses paid. While attending college, she reintroduced herself to her father and found him smart and charming, and she continued to thrive academically. After graduation, she was hired by a local television station.

A larger income helped her to continue supporting her children and to purchase a home so they could visit more frequently. "I'd tried getting them back when they were younger, but their grandmother fought it. Still, they were never out of my life; they'd come for summers and holidays. But they'd heard all this negative stuff about me from their father's family. My son believed I didn't love him because I hadn't raised him. And when he was fourteen, he announced to the family that he was gay. I have to admit that we put him put down for it. His grandmother beat him over the head with a Bible."

As for her private life, Marilyn admits she was sexually promiscuous. "I later learned that some people who are abused use sex as a conquering tool. When I was little, I couldn't control what was happening with my stepfather. As I grew older, being promiscuous made me feel I was in charge of the sex." She enjoyed drinking too, and was driving home from a bar when her car was hit by a drunk driver. "My car rolled over an embankment. I hadn't been religious, but at that moment, I said, 'Jesus, help me.' A voice in my head told me to be calm." The car was totaled, the convertible top smashed as flat as a pancake, but she crawled from the car, unscathed. The next day, after sharing details of the crash with a minister, she was led to Christ.

Her deepening faith didn't mean that life progressed smoothly, but it helped her through a terrible ordeal. Her son died at twenty-two from an undiagnosed heart condition. "He had lived with me for a little while and I thanked God that we had a chance to get close. A friend had told me about a gay man who died and how no one in his family came to his funeral. That scared me to death. A lot of gay people have to make their own family because they get rejected. I didn't want that for my son. When he was twenty-one, I'd called him for his birthday. I said, 'I want you to know that you're my son and I love you.' He said it was the best gift he'd ever had for his birthday."

Not long after Marilyn buried her son, her daughter announced that she wanted nothing to do with her and refused to speak to her. She accused her mother of abandoning her. Years passed before the two were reconciled.

So, as you can see, Marilyn had experienced many losses by the time her second husband walked out. And although she'd excelled at school and work, she was still struggling with her past as a victim of sexual abuse. In one of the best books to address the subject, *No Secrets, No Lies: How Black Families Can Heal from Sexual Abuse*, author Robin D. Stone writes of women like Marilyn. "We have buried sexual abuse so deep into our psyches that we would never connect it to today's physical illness and pain, our depression or addiction, our inability to hold a job, get out of debt, find satisfaction in a relationship, nurture our children, or simply say no to people or situations that do us harm."

Marilyn considered herself pretty tough, but, after her husband's abandonment, "If I'd ever had a period of depression that was it." She didn't have qualms about turning to a psychologist. As she points out, "God sent Luke the physician to help Paul."

I agree with her decision to seek professional help. God does give some people gifts that can help us heal. From my point of view, not seeking a release from pain and waiting for God to heal it is akin to emptying a bag of corn kernels on an open field and asking God to make it grow. *We* are God's hands. Marilyn found an African American woman, a licensed psychotherapist, to help her restore her life. Talk therapy has been found to be tremendously effective in relieving the symptoms of depression.

Marilyn says, "This woman said something really important to me. I was crying about losing my husband, and told her, 'I thought he was really different.' She said, 'You thought he was different, but from what you've told me, they were all the same men with different faces. They were all physically or emotionally abusive.' "

During months of therapy Marilyn worked on the issues of sexual violation and her heart-wrenching guilt concerning her children. After a year and a half, she decided to sell her house and attend graduate school in Boston. She has since relocated to Philadelphia, and has found a church home. "I was driving by looking for an apartment and I passed a Baptist Church. It turned out to be the best place for me."

That's also where she met her current husband, a business executive. She credits her therapy with helping her attract a man who truly loves her back. If you phone their home, he answers in a deep baritone and offers a warm greeting. Handing the phone to Marilyn, he says, "It's for you, honey." They're simple words, but for a woman who once thirsted for kind words, they're like balm from Gilead.

He and Marilyn were friends for a few years, but their relationship deepened when he insisted on accompanying her to visit an ailing aunt. "My aunt eventually regained her speech and began telling

me that he was wonderful. He and I began studying the Bible to-
gether. We still do. And we spend a lot of time praying together."
It would not be a matter of putting words in her mouth to say that
Marilyn feels blessed. She is, and she lives like it.

It you're struggling with depression, I urge you to seek help, particularly if you have entertained any suicidal thoughts. If you do see a
therapist, ask God to bless your actions. Dr. Wade says emotional
energy is directly tied to our spirituality. "A therapist can help you
clear up places that have been siphoning off energy. Therapy can
help you create a space for energy to flow through. Once that energy
is no longer pressed down, there's room for an even deeper connection to God."

Resources
- Dr. Brenda Wade, who practices in San Francisco,
  California, can be reached via e-mail at
  Docwade@docwade.com.
- Voices in Action. This organization provides referrals for
  therapeutic help and support groups: (800) 786-4238,
  www.voices-action.org.
- Survivors of Incest Anonymous. This referral line can offer
  information on twelve-step recovery programs in your
  vicinity: (410) 893-3322, www.siawso.org.

In the next chapter, you'll find suggestions that will help you continue to take positive steps toward living your blessings.

CHAPTER 10

Naming the Blessings

One of my most vivid childhood memories is of my father, Wilbert T. Johnson, setting aside time each and every evening to thank our Lord and Savior for the many blessings in his life. There I was, a little girl, seeing this beloved man, so big and strong and powerful, in a position of supplication: on his knees, head bent, and palms pressed together as he elucidated his many and varied blessings. This nightly devotion served as a powerful lesson to me about the importance of praising the Lord, of naming the blessings as a way of recharging one's emotional energy, so that we can become a force to be reckoned with.

As the years passed, my father seemed to have more and more to be grateful for, and one business venture in particular prospered. In 1962, with $1,000 in savings, he and my mother founded the Johnson Security Bureau. Almost from the start, business skyrocketed as he supplied security personnel to local concerns—everything from supermarkets to Catholic bazaars and weekly bingo games. The family-owned business gave me an opportunity to see firsthand the tremendous self-sacrifice that was required, and how it could eat away at a person's time. Dad was never too busy to pray, however. (Let me pause to point out that my mother was also prayerfully powerful, often praising God as the source from whom all blessings flow.)

My father's daily prayers were a way of acting on what he believed to be a spiritual obligation: "In everything give thanks, for this is the will of God in Christ Jesus for you" (I Thessalonians 5:18). Of course I wasn't privy to exactly what Dad was saying, but I'm sure that among many things, he praised God for the opportunity to start the business, for the contracts that kept it afloat, and for each and every worker and their families. Today the Johnson Security Bureau employs as many as three hundred individuals and was recently cited as the longest running black-owned family business in the Bronx.

I'm not suggesting that the enterprise prospered solely because of my father's gratitude. There are proprietors and professionals of every stripe who wouldn't consider thanking anyone but themselves for their success, but who still manage to turn impressive profits. We've all heard the expression, "God helps those who help themselves." It's important to remind people that God also helps those who can't help themselves.

Here's the trick about praising God: We don't do it just *for* God; He wants us to do it for ourselves. Learning to praise the Lord is a spiritual discipline that reaps rewards, according to Robert Emmons, Ph.D., a psychologist who pioneered a study of gratitude and coauthored *Words of Gratitude: For Mind, Body, and Soul.* Dr. Emmons writes, "The more grateful we are, the more reasons we have to be grateful. This knowledge can create a shift from gratitude as a response to gratitude as an attitude, as a receptive state that allows blessings to flow in . . . this attitude brings about a relationship with the Divine, the source from which all good comes."

Studying gratitude in the psychology department of the University of California, Davis, Dr. Emmons and his colleagues found that people who tend to express gratitude report high levels of alertness and energy and are likely to be engaged in social behaviors that involve helping others. "Not only do they feel good, they also did good," he writes. Compared to those who seldom express gratitude, he found that grateful people tend to be better at coping with problems, enjoy better health, and are more socially adaptable.

Dr. Emmons's research confirmed what so many people have long sensed: that praising God makes us feel better by revving up our energy level. That's all the more reason to follow the call to: "Bless the Lord, O My soul, and forget not all his benefits" (Psalm 103:2). Praising God makes the colors of spring seem brighter. Praising God makes food tastier and more satisfying. Praising God, even on the chilliest nights, makes us feel warmer, more comforted. Gratitude helps us feel the fullness and joy of life.

The healed leper in Luke understood the joy of gratitude. After Jesus had healed ten lepers, only one returned to thank Him. "And one of them, when he saw that he was healed, turned back, and with a loud voice, glorified God, and fell down on his face at his feet, giving him thanks; and he was a Samaritan. And Jesus answering said, 'Were there not ten cleansed? But where are the nine?' " (Luke 17:15–17).

Let's get this straight from the start. Jesus wasn't asking for praise and gratitude for himself. He wasn't an insecure gift-giver who got puffed up with self-concern when people kneeled at his feet. The Lord is perfect and self-contained. He can't be manipulated into giving us what we feel we need because we praise Him. He fills our lives with gifts because He loves us. He sacrificed His life for us because He loves us.

If there was ever proof that the Lord wants us to learn gratitude for our own sakes, consider the celebrities and multimillionaires plastered on the front pages of newspapers and magazines and featured on television shows. These are people who drive the biggest cars, live in posh neighborhoods, and carry credit cards that seem to have no limit, and yet, we can tell by their actions that despite their wealth, they often feel spiritually destitute, empty, null, and void. Some will take drugs, hoping to fill up the spaces. Others will drink to drown out their troubles. They may shop 'til they drop, and isn't that the truth, because the only thing going down is them: They feel more deprived, more resentful, more negative and gloomy.

Lee's oldest son, Paul, twenty-seven, learned about gratitude from the other way around. An internship at a restaurant was one of his graduation requirements at the California-based culinary school he attended. He moved to New York and landed an unpaid job that allowed him to train under one of the most highly recognized chefs in the city. As the low man on the totem pole, Paul was often subjected to this chef's selfish, angry tirades. Despite this atmosphere of ingratitude, Paul worked hard. At the end of the three-month internship, when the chef asked Paul to continue working for free, the young man, somewhat embittered, refused, and moved back to California. Paul found a good job at a restaurant, but after a year of working for a contentious manager, Paul was fired.

Out of the blue, the very next day, Paul's mother ran into the chef from the New York restaurant, and this chef began singing Paul's praises and asking her to tell her son if he ever wanted to come back, there was always a paid position waiting at his restaurant. Paul didn't want to move back to the Big Apple, but he did want to capitalize on the chance meeting by writing a letter to the chef asking for a letter of reference that would help him secure another job. As Paul wrote to the chef, something strange happened. He knew that if he was going to ask the man for a favor, he'd better start out by praising the chef, and he did. He wrote about how much he'd learned working under him, and as he began to list what he'd learned in detail, Paul felt himself relaxing. Any residual resentment he'd felt about this chef's mistreatment began to fade away. He also found himself shaking off the anxiety he'd felt about finding another job. By praising the chef, Paul realized how blessed he'd been to work under this man. And *then*, he asked for the letter of reference. And so it is with God. Gratitude prepares us for a relationship with the Almighty.

Showing gratitude is a beautiful thing. It builds energy, gathers momentum, stirs people up and makes them want to start something, do something good. We who are grateful to the Lord know we couldn't exist without Him. But simply knowing is not sufficient, not if we want to keep a positive balance. At least one major corporation seems aware of this fact. Witness the advertising campaign of an international bank whose slogan states: "We don't say thank you, we *do* thank you."

The decision makers at the top of that megabank recognized that the only way to keep ahead of the competition and boost profits was to generate energy from within by reminding their employees that without their customers they would cease to exist. The marketing managers knew they could create more employee loyalty, more customer satisfaction with their newest slogan: "Let the thanking begin."

I say hallelujah to that idea, and I'm going to say it again, "Let the thanking begin." That's what we do at Believers Christian Fellowship, the church I pastor that relocated in 2004 to Harlem. And maybe it's the same at your parish. Several minutes before the service begins, a Praise Team comes out. This team is comprised of five to seven people blessed with musical and singing talent, and they get the energy rolling among the early attendees by proclaiming the good news about our crucified, risen, and soon returning King. They're like an advance team that warms up a crowd before a politician comes out to speak, gets them cheering and clapping, energized and ready to hear the Lord's word.

I am grateful and say many prayers of thanks for our Praise Team, for once they've performed, by the time I come out, I can feel a force of energy in that sanctuary. Minutes earlier, people might have walked in feeling burdened by their cares. They may have walked in intending to ask God's help in getting their marriages straight, or calming wild teenagers, or coming up with rent money, or passing the next big exam. And there's not a thing wrong with them asking.

God never grows weary of our cries for help. He encouraged his disciples to always pray and never give up (Luke 18:1). He urges us to devote ourselves to prayer (Colossians 4:2). He promises to bring about justice for those who cry out to him day and night (Luke 18:7–8). And even when we're too weary to utter the words, He promises that the spirit will intercede with groans that words cannot express (Romans 8:26). But before we ask for help, He asks for something from us. Before our prayers and petitions, He asks for words of thanksgiving (Philippians 4:6).

And this is how the ministry of the Praise Team works at Believers Christian Fellowship. Their words and songs of praise, the gratitude they generate among the congregation puts people in a state that makes them more receptive to the blessings. Suddenly it's no longer a building housing individual minds that are focused on their own problems, but a congregation focused on the glory of God. The worshippers are no longer just an assembly of individuals but one church, built on one foundation of Jesus Christ our Lord.

These parishioners have found that gratitude and praise help generate the energy that can help us live like we're blessed. It will help create the aspects of blessed that we have covered in Parts I, II, and III: the balance, the love, and the energy that is necessary to bring about radical change. Expressing gratitude gets us down on our knees, even if only mentally, with our heads bent and hands pressed together.

Some people prefer to wait until they're in pastoral settings, perhaps sitting by a beautiful body of water or looking out on a springtime field of flowers. As for me, I don't want to wait for a beautiful environment. I thank the Lord whether I'm sitting in my car stuck in traffic, amid blaring horns, or at the doctor's office waiting to hear about the results of my mammogram. Like any form of prayer, I know that the more I praise God the better I'll feel.

Katherine, a thirty-year-old historian, knows about praising the Lord even during difficult times. She smiles with pleasure as she recalls finally reaching a point in her fifteen-year marriage when she and her husband were both earning more and could finally start saving. When they had a tidy sum put away, they were hit with a problem that caused them to spend every penny of their savings, a problem that eventually put them into debt and zapped their future earnings for the next several years. The family was shocked by their sudden change of circumstances. They'd always been a praying family and during this period they prayed even more. But there was some resistance when Katherine said at one of their family prayer sessions, "I want to thank God for our financial hardships."

She later explained that she wasn't suggesting that God had caused their troubles. She understood that God only brings about good, never adversity. But she reminded her family of the promise that "All things work together for good to them that love God, to them who are the called according to His purpose" (Romans 8:28). She told them that she trusted God enough to believe that with His help, they could make something good of their troubles. Five years later, she knows just what that good was.

"For years, the biggest obstacle for me and my husband was our different attitudes about money. It wasn't as simple as he hated spending and I spent everything, but we were definitely a contrast in styles, and this caused many conflicts between us, and our kids knew this because we argued, loudly. But I believe our prayers and love of God helped us make something good out of those years on a financial edge. By necessity, I had to start cutting back drastically. I came up with all kinds of cost-saving measures. We had to watch every cent. It took about two years into our financial troubles before I noticed that my husband and I had stopped arguing over money. I will always trust God to comfort me when something terrible occurs and to work through me for the good. I'll always praise His name."

A few other people were asked to share their thoughts on developing attitudes of gratitude. Jane G. Ravarra, eighty-four, who worked as a receptionist for thirty-three years in the prosecutor's division of the Wayne County, Michigan, criminal justice system, praises God dozens of times in a given day.

Ravarra says, "As soon as my eyes fly open and my tail lifts up, I say 'Thank you, Lord.' I had surgery recently and my niece was with me, but it was frightening to know that I was going through a door and didn't know what was waiting for me on the other side. Praising God made a difference. I thanked Him for guiding me through every step of my life. People like to think they deserve what they get. But there's a difference between having a talent and having a gift. If you take sewing class and get good at making clothes, that's a talent. If you sit down in front of a piano for the first time and you touch the keys and make a musical sound, that's a gift and that's from God. He's waiting for us to discover our gifts. He gives them graciously. I am grateful for the gifts that I've identified and those which have not yet been revealed. And for that, I thank Him."

Closer to home, my husband, Ronald Cook, responded to a question about what he felt grateful for in the moment. He said, "I thank God for my family. God is good. At the moment, many of the people I care about are enjoying a reasonable portion of health and strength. Thank you, Lord. I'm grateful that I can contribute to this world we live in. I'm grateful for my wife. I praise God for leading me to someone with whom every day is an adventure. I'm grateful that she can travel all over the country to spread the word and no danger or harm has come to her. Thank you, Lord. I'm grateful that I have a job, working at Convent Avenue church as an administrator. I'd do this for free if I could, and so I praise you for my position. If there is loss in my future, I intend to keep my head high, praising God and telling Him that I'm willing to receive whatever He has for me."

It's no coincidence that this chapter began with an image of my father praising God and then closing with my husband's words of gratitude. They are two of those strong and wonderful black men that statistics tell us no longer exist. I thank God for helping me to ignore the naysayers and for giving me vision that helps us see the divine reality. God's creation is bountiful, and in this moment, for this I praise Him.

Ten Ways to Cultivate an Attitude of Gratitude

1. Morning devotions. Get in the habit of praying every morning before you walk out the door. Whether you are single, are married, or have children, use these moments to lower your head and thank the Lord (in advance) for taking you through the day. Thank the Lord for the job you are about to perform. Thank God for allowing you to make a positive difference in the world. If you're praying with schoolchildren, thank God for their teachers and their school.

2. Praise book. Carry a small notebook and throughout the day make a list of all you're grateful for and praise God for each of these.

3. Listen to yourself. As you converse with others notice whether most of your comments are laced with complaints. Don't scold yourself if you hear yourself complaining, but do explore whether there is anything good that might come out of a difficult situation.

4. The right words. Get in the habit of thanking people for even the smallest services. Remember that we're all made in God's image. When we're kind to others, we are thanking God for the human creation. And saying thank you to those who assist us is a way of acknowledging their worth.

5. Volunteer time. I know that I mentioned this in the last chapter, but it bears repeating: Find some way to utilize those God-given gifts by sharing with others.

6. Little things. Know those beat-up slippers that you slide into at the end of the day? That's right, they're almost worn to a nub, but don't they feel good? Learn to thank God for the small things and you'll start seeing the world through new eyes.

7. Posting a quote. Copy this quote and tape it to your mirror or on your dashboard or refrigerator as a reminder to praise the Lord: "It is a good thing to give thanks unto the Lord, to sing praises unto thy name, O most High: to show forth thy loving kindness in the morning and thy faithfulness every night. Upon an instrument of ten strings, and upon the psaltery; upon the harp with a solemn sound. For thou, Lord, has made me glad through thy work: I will triumph in the works of thy hands. O Lord, how great are thy works! And thy thoughts are very deep" (Psalm 92:1–5).

8. Check energy drops. When you are feeling low, your energy level is dipping. Rev it up by praising the Lord. The more energy you invest in the moment, the more empowered you will feel.

9. Elder care. Develop a relationship with a sick or shut-in elderly person. Even if you can only find time to send occasional greeting cards or phone on weekends, know that these are precious moments for the lonely, and you're sure to hear a thank you. Accept the gratitude on behalf of the Lord.

10. Evening devotions. The end of the day is a good time to praise God for all He has done. If you're not doing this, it's a great habit to start. If you do it already, keep it up!

PART IV

B
L
E
S **Spirit**
S
E
D

CHAPTER 11

Forgiving Seventy Times Seven

lthough sometimes confused with energy, the emotions that motivate us to live fully, spirit—the first *S* in "blessed"—is God's awesome power. This life force, which surrounds us and lives within us, is a vital requirement for those of us who want to live as if we're blessed. The presence of the Holy Spirit within us is one of our greatest gifts, for we are promised that "the fruit of the Spirit is love, joy, peace, longsuffering, kindness, goodness, faithfulness, gentleness, self-control" (Galatians 5:22–23). These qualities can empower us to achieve the unimaginable, and thus, compel us to learn about the care and handling of our inner spirit.

Maintaining a relationship with our inner spirit requires that we never neglect it or allow it to grow cold. If you think I sound as if I'm referring to keeping a fire stoked, you're right. Paul compared God's spirit to an ember in a fire and urged Timothy to stir it up and fan it into flames. Of course prayer and expressions of gratitude, along with other suggestions offered in this work, will help maintain your spiritual relationship. Tapping into your highest self, however, requires bringing this work up a notch.

Just as the buildup of clutter in your home signals that it's time for a spring cleaning, and just as that rumble in the car's engine indicates that it's time for a tune-up, there's a way of knowing when you're in need of a spiritual cleansing. The key sign is whether you've been able to forgive those who have hurt you. Don't shrug off the idea. Simply saying you've forgiven someone is not the same as actually forgiving. Holding on to resentments is human. That's why Jesus taught us to pray: "Forgive us our sins as we forgive those who sin against us." He was reminding us of our contract with God. He will forgive us for hurting Him by sinning, if we can forgive those who have hurt us. It's not like he minced words on the subject. When Peter asked him how often he should forgive, Jesus replied, "Seventy times seven" (Matthew 18:21–22). He meant that our forgiveness should be boundless.

I urge you to fight your way through denial about forgiving past transgressions. Remaining spiritually strong requires letting go of past grievances. I know it's not easy, and in fact, I've found forgiveness to be among the most challenging of spiritual disciplines. It helps to remember that lack of forgiveness is so powerful it can destroy love. Hatred and resentment are so consuming they can douse the flames of the most fiery inner spirits. Unforgiveness manifests itself in our bodies and can make us ill.

Many of my parishioners know this, and in their determination to be good Christians, they often turn to me for help in learning to forgive. They can be tough on themselves because they want to be able to forgive and forget. So they're surprised when I tell them that forgiving is recommended, but that they should never forget. They may be stunned to hear this from their pastor because they recall God's own sterling example: "For I will forgive their iniquity, and their sin I will remember no more" (Jeremiah 31:34).

I thank God with all my heart for His perfection. He is able to forgive and forget my sins. And that poses a dilemma. We humans do sin, and we are imperfect, which is why we can't afford to forget who injured us and how. Forgetting could mean leaving ourselves or loves ones open to more pain. The only way we can protect ourselves or others is to remember how we were hurt, so we can avoid future injury.

Rather than forgetting, we can keep the fires of our inner spirit burning by learning to forgive. At the end of this chapter I offer specific steps for entering into the forgiveness process. You'll know that you've reached your goal when you can remember the experience without triggering past hurts. Ridding your life of resentments can lighten your load.

Madison De La Burre of New Orleans learned at an early age that anger and resentment have real consequences in our lives. At twenty-nine she still possesses the long, lean body that made her a successful model. But what's most surprising about her is not that she's so lovely, but that her experiences have not left her with a hardened heart. "A lot of people grow up without their fathers," Madison points out. "My mother had me at sixteen, and then my father abandoned us. When it was just me and Mom it was great. We'd go to the movies and to the park. We had fun."

Her family's troubles began after Madison's mother married, had three more children, and was subsequently abandoned by this man. "My mother is Haitian and speaks French; she never learned to speak English. And she stayed home to care for me and my siblings, so she didn't have any job experience. After my stepfather left her with four kids to feed, she was in trouble. Then she met this woman across the street from us, who introduced her to drugs. My mother started partying with her and left me to take care of the kids."

Ten years older than her youngest sibling, Madison dropped out of school to care for them. Somehow they managed to get by for a few years, barely surviving on the minimum wage that her mother earned through infrequent jobs. "My mother came up with an idea about moving into a women's shelter and putting us up for temporary custody. I told her that we should all go to a shelter together or that maybe she could go into rehab and I would continue taking care of the kids. I was afraid of our family getting split up. My little sister and brothers were like my own kids, but my mother wouldn't listen to me." By that time, when Madison was fourteen, her mother was using heroin and crack cocaine. "I begged her to change her mind about the shelter. I was afraid we'd never see her again, but she'd called a social worker, who told her to bring us down."

Madison remembers the cold sterility of the social services office. "My mom was in one office talking to the social worker, the kids were outside playing, and I was waiting out in the hall. All of a sudden something told me to go and check on the kids. I was still pretty short, but I stood on my toes and looked through this tiny glass window. I saw a man taking the kids by the hand and leading them toward a car. I ran back to the office for help, pounded at the door, yelling at my mom: 'Someone's taking the kids.' This social worker started telling me how this was for the best, and that since I was older, they couldn't place me with my siblings; that I had to be sent someplace for older children, even though they'd promised to keep us together."

Madison raced after the car that was transporting her siblings from her life. "Their little faces were pressed against the back window. I didn't get a chance to say goodbye." Her eyes filled with tears as she remembers that day, and then she recalls her anger.

Back in the office, after demanding that the children be returned, Madison exploded. She threw chairs and broke windows. "I bit that lady. I hit her. I kicked her in the shin. I made a big mess. They had to restrain me and they gave me sedatives."

She awoke in a group home, several miles outside of New Orleans. "I didn't know where my family was. I stayed there for a couple of months, but I was small and there were so many bullies. One day I stole some money from the office, grabbed the photograph I had of my siblings, and I ran away."

Unaccustomed to traveling on her own, Madison took several days to return to the city. "I slept in train stations and alleyways, on rooftops, and one time beside a pigeon coop. I only had a few dollars, so I'd watch people coming out of fast food restaurants, and ate what they threw away. I begged a man at a restaurant for food but he told me to get the fuck away from him. Another time, I walked through a tunnel at night and these boys chased me. One of them grabbed the chain around my neck, but I pulled away." Determined to locate her family, Madison eventually returned to her old neighborhood, but was unable to learn anything about their whereabouts.

For a teenage girl living on her own life was not easy. She checked herself into a group home, but was sexually abused. So she took to sleeping at a bus station. She continued to search for her siblings while the social worker refused to divulge their location. During her frenzied search, Madison did learn the whereabouts of her biological father, but it turned out that after a disagreement with his new wife he had moved to another state.

Finally, when Madison was eighteen, a sympathetic social worker heard about her plight and arranged a reunion with her mother. "Mom was in a shelter. I don't think I would have recognized her. She was so thin from doing drugs. Her face was scarred and she'd had syphilis and had been raped. She was glad to see me, but she wasn't really there. She started crying, begging me to take her home with me."

By then Madison was starting to earn enough from modeling to support her mother, and she acceded to her request. "I was able to forgive her, because I told myself it was the drugs that led her to make bad choices. I blamed the drugs, not her. She went into rehab and stopped using."

With her mother back in her life, Madison was able to track down her siblings. Four years had passed, but Madison found that they were still together, living in foster care. "They hadn't forgiven us for abandoning them," Madison says. "The youngest one asked my mom, 'Why did you take so long to come and get us?' I was glad to see them and proud. They were so beautiful."

Madison's mom still had visitation rights and slowly the family started on the delicate path of getting to know one another again. Their relationship seemed to be moving in the right direction until Madison's mother relapsed and began using drugs again. "We had a court hearing coming up about the kids, but I had to work. I told Mom to get it postponed. She didn't do it. She went to see the social worker on her own. This woman probably realized she was high. She got Mom to sign some papers."

A week later, when Madison and her mother showed up for their weekly visitation, they learned disappointing news. "My mother had signed away her rights to the kids. They'd been adopted and taken away. We went to court to get them back, but we lost. I've never seen them again."

Bitter and disappointed, Madison moved away. Her life didn't progress as she'd planned. One night at a party, someone offered her drugs and she tried them. Before long she was addicted. "I sniffed heroin and then I got into freebasing. I eventually went to jail, where I was raped and beaten. I was stabbed and shot."

After her release, she met a man who'd also done time, and like her, had become a devoted Christian and was determined to never go back to prison. They started a life together, but not before Madison did the one thing she needed to do to thrive: She forgave her mother.

"I don't believe in judging anyone. I'll leave that to God. If I'm still in this world after so much has happened to me, I know God's looking out for me. My mom loves my fiancé. We live together and have a good life. If I hadn't forgiven her, I could never have rested in peace."

Madison forgave her mother because that was the only route to true salvation. She knew that her mother was precious to the Lord and that when Jesus died for our sins, He wasn't excluding anyone from that list. He died for all of us. She knew that as long as her heart remained hardened toward her mother, she was living out her grief over her lost siblings and the loss of her own childhood.

By taking drugs, she realized, she'd been shackled to her mother's past. Drugs were Madison's way of trying to forget rather than for-give. When we forgive it helps us, not necessarily the other person. By forgiving, Madison freed herself and was able to move on. That was why after all her terrible experiences she still seems so alive. One look at her radiant smile and it becomes obvious that she is in pos-session of the fruits of God's forgiveness: love, tenderness, compas-sion, and humility.

Madison says of her life today: "I love going home to my mom and my fiancé. We're very close." In fact, the three of them make that family she'd always wanted.

As Madison's story suggests, the closer we are to someone the more they have the power to wound us. Sometimes the hurt inflicted oc-curs over a long period of time, causing resentment to build up. That's what happened with Carol Reed of Chicago, who met her husband, Al, in 1941, when she was all of nineteen, a slip of a girl, standing on State Street, bemoaning the fact that her sister's car had broken down.

"I can't remember if it was engine trouble or a flat tire, but I do remember Al walking up to us. He was so tall and handsome in his Marine uniform. He offered to assist us. We fell in love right away."

They married right away too, and moved to North Carolina. Al was one of the first African American men accepted into the segre-gated branch of the Marines, and was subject to racist belittling from the white officers. Al remained civil but demanded that they show him respect. "He was a very proud man, and when he felt he was being treated unjustly he spoke up," Carol says. Although this kind of attitude is not generally acceptable in the military, it didn't harm Al's career. He served with distinction during World War II, and for another two decades in the military.

In the sixties, the family, which eventually included three sons, resettled in Chicago, and Al was hired as one of the first black managers of a major plant. "It was a great job, but Al drew the line at being misused by anyone. The workers respected him. He was proud that he'd been a Marine. He didn't wear his uniform anymore, of course, but it was hanging in the closet, intact. His workers called him Sarge. At home he was a role model for our sons. He was so involved with them."

Ten years into the job, however, a white truck driver punched Al, and when Al struck back, a supervisor told him that he should have "done a Martin Luther King and turned the other cheek." Just like that, Al was fired.

"It tore him apart," Carol says. Determined to keep working, he accepted menial jobs. But he was unable to get over what had happened to him, and he was unable to forgive and move on. "Our lives changed from the day he was fired," Carol says. "I prayed for change, but he became depressed, started drinking. He became a different man."

He also became more possessive of Carol. "His pride was hurt and he was feeling insecure. I'd started working at a grocery store and my new manager, a young man, became good friends with my husband. This man really looked up to him. Al would barbecue and he'd come by with his girlfriends, and he really enjoyed our boys."

When her manager was promoted and moved across the state to a district job, Carol hoped the father-and-son relationship would continue between this man and her husband, but Al's growing inse-curities caused a permanent rift between them.

"I got a phone call from this young man at work. I was excited to hear from him, until he started to ask me what I'd told my husband. I didn't know what he was talking about until I learned that Al had somehow gotten the idea that this man had some interest in me other than friendship. He'd accused this man and then suggested that I'd admitted to it. Of course I hadn't. Nothing had happened between us. It was damaging. This young man had gotten married and Al had spread the rumor so that his wife heard about it. This young man was furious, and I was hurt and humiliated."

Al's inability to forgive those who had hurt him had changed their life for the worse. Carol was at a point of no return. She had tolerated Al's heavy drinking, intensifying jealousy, boisterous and angry temper tantrums, but she was unwilling to take further humil-iation. "We still had one son left at home, but I told Al I wanted our marriage to end. When he refused to move from the house, I took our son and moved into an apartment. I left everything else be-hind. The only thing I took was clothes and one pot. The boys were all very upset and I was brokenhearted."

Though she had moved out, Carol encouraged her sons to honor their father. "I told them, 'If you're short of time and you have to choose who you'll visit, go to him.' I wanted them to remember that he'd been a good father."

Over the years, heavy drinking took a toll on Al's health, and di-abetes and a failing heart left him confined to a wheelchair. Carol consulted with the Lord and then knew just what to do.

"I started stopping by the house every day to see if there was any-thing Al wanted. I cleaned his house and drove him to doctor's appointments, made sure he was all right. One day he told me he wanted to borrow money on the house, but that the woman at the bank said that a loan would require my signature. I went to the bank with him to sign, and once we explained that we were separated, the bank manager couldn't believe it. She warned Al that this would make it easier for me to get the house from him if he didn't pay the note. He looked at me and told her, 'Carol would never do anything to hurt me.' I knew that was his way of apologizing for wrecking our marriage."

One day, Al asked Carol why she was so good to him. "I told him, 'Because you need me.' " Days later, one of her sons phoned to say that Al had died in his sleep. Al was laid to rest in a military funeral, with full honors. Carol was grateful to God that she hadn't let her resentment cause a rift in the family.

She stood at Al's grave and knew that she'd forgiven him. "I stopped picturing him as someone who was angry and loud, and reminded myself of what he'd been like on that first day when I saw him, when he came to my rescue, that tall, handsome Marine. That's how you forgive people, by remembering who they were at their best."

Here are some more suggestions that can help you remain in the spirit, working your way through to a point of forgiveness.

I. Write it down. On a slip of paper, write about how you were hurt and your fantasies of revenge, and include thoughts on how you'd like to even the score. Don't try to be polite. Write fast and furiously and let it rip. Now release the anger. When you've finished writing, burn this slip of paper or tear it into tiny pieces and flush it away. Tell yourself that it's over. Remember Paul saying in Philippians 3:13–14, "Forgetting the things which are behind, . . . I press on toward the goal unto the prize of the high calling of God." In other words, release it, and look to God in prayer.

2. Write in your journal. Ask yourself whether you have ever denied the seriousness of the offense or blamed yourself. If you have, use your soothing internal voice to comfort yourself.

3. Decide to forgive. This is a choice that you get to make.

4. Pray. Ask God for assistance in forgiving and allow the Holy Spirit to work through you. You'll know you're closing in on your goal when you can comfortably ask the Heavenly Father to lift this person in prayer.

5. Check in with yourself. If you are struggling with forgiving, continue to take time out for journal writing, exploring the ways your resentment has hurt you and others.

CHAPTER 12

Maximizing Your Creative Spirit

I'm going to start this chapter in an unusual way...by asking you to put this book down, for the moment at least. Before you do, however, let me explain. I'd like you to open your Bible to the beginning, to Genesis, and take your time reading aloud if possible the first and second accounts of creation, ending with 2:24. Please start now.

If you have just finished your reading of Genesis, perhaps those last words, "and they were not ashamed" linger in your memory. To me, those five words help me imagine Adam and Eve as trusting, childlike, and jubilant over the beauty of God's creation. Those words "and they were not ashamed" go directly to my inner core, to that place where I feel no need to be perfect, no need to strike a certain pose or speak in the right tones; a place where I feel no judgment from myself or others, an emotionally safe place. Some describe this kind of euphoria as "getting happy," and that's all right with me, because when I read the creation stories I *am* happy and childlike, and thrilled by the mighty power of the Lord, our God and Savior.

In fact, I hope you will allow yourself to step into this same space, right beside me, where someone might truthfully say of you, "and she was not ashamed." Go on, take God's hand and step down without fear of failing or falling. Shake off feelings of self-consciousness and allow the words "Thank you, Lord" to burst from your lips.

In this space, you can experience God's creative power by picturing the miracle of His creation. From a formless void He created the heavens and the earth, hallelujah. He separated the light from the darkness and the waters from dry land, hallelujah. He covered the earth with vegetation: "Herbs yielding seed after their kind, and trees bearing fruit" (Genesis 1:12). And He saw that it was good, but He didn't rest there. By the end of the fourth day He had created the great lights of the sun and the moon, and as the week continued, birds and fish and "everything that creeps upon the ground of every kind." Hallelujah! Isn't God good. I didn't forget the question mark on that sentence. I *know* He's good. And I know *you know* He's good.

He's so good that He could have stopped right then and there with the miracle of His creation. But He didn't. He created man and woman. He created humankind. He created us and connected our life to His with His breath. That's why I asked you to read both creation accounts, because the second story fills in the details about our uniqueness. "God formed man from the dust of the ground, and breathed into his nostrils the breath of life; and the man became a living being" (Genesis 2:7).

I want to pause momentarily to examine something of tremendous importance pertaining to the creativity theme of this chapter, as a continuation of the exploration of spirit, the first *S* in "blessed." Our bodies are, of course, the temples of God's spirit. After molding our forms, He blessed us with the "breath of life." But just what does that mean? We know that long ago, whether people were writing in Hebrew, Greek, or Latin, they used the same word for "breath," "wind," and "spirit." They knew that like the wind, God's spirit is an invisible, mighty force.

Picture God shaping Adam from the dust, and when you imagine Him breathing into that lifeless form, erase the image of one of those white-jacketed doctors administering oxygen from *ER*. Don't compare the scene to someone giving mouth-to-mouth resuscitation on one of those beach patrol shows. Those shows portray actors pretending to keep someone from dying. Genesis is about life, not death. It's the real deal here, and we're talking about the Almighty, the Everlasting, the Lord God, the Great Creator. He wasn't just keeping someone alive, he was *making* someone come alive, bringing someone to life. God was infusing Adam with His spirit, with His invisible, powerful creative force.

We aren't self-centered enough to forget that we weren't the only living, breathing beings that He created. We know from Genesis that God loves the animals he created. That's reason enough to cherish them and treat them with kindness and respect. As it says of the animals in Genesis 1:22, "God blessed them."

In that same book though, you'll also find another significant truth. God made humankind unique in all of nature. We know this not simply because he gave us dominion over the animals, and not even solely because he breathed his life force into us. We know of our creative uniqueness because among all living things, He gave us the power to name: "And whatever the man called every living creature, that was its name" (2:19).

The fact that a human being could name the other animals helps us understand that God intended for us to share elements of His creative spirit. Adam was able to name things because God gave us the gift of language, a way of communicating thoughts and ideas. Language is the basis for creation. Let me explain what I mean. Of course we aren't the only animals that communicate with one another. Take the groundhog for example. For the sake of survival, a groundhog may grunt and bend its head to indicate to a mate that it has found eatable buried roots in a particular spot. We humans, on the other hand, blessed with the capacity for language, might simply call to a mate, "Honey, I found roots here, and the soil is moist, so if we look around we might find a riverbed, and this might be a good spot to build a house." Through language, we expand the power of knowledge in a condensed form.

As a result, while other animals must adapt to their natural habitats to survive, we alone have the language skills to pass on information so we can make things from nature—create—in essence adjusting nature to ourselves. Thanks to our gift of language and because we house God's creative spirit, humans have invented wheels to traverse long distances. Because of the gift of language, humans have learned to pass on information about the usefulness of fire—which is from nature—and rather than having to wait for lightning to strike, we've created a technology that makes fire available when we need it.

We don't simply use our creative gifts to communicate the vast amounts of information required for our survival. We look around at the beauty and plentitude and notice that the river sparkles with the radiance of the sun. We dance in joy, mimicking the movement of the leafy boughs stirred by the invisible force of the wind. We create music and art and poetry as a reflection of the beauty of God's creation and to enhance our environment. And when we live blessed lives we use our creativity to enhance God's creation in the knowledge that using our creativity is a way of returning the favor to God. Our creative output may be seen in everything from the preparation of an appealing and delicious meal to the sewing of a quilt or needlepoint to the design and construction of a lovely home by the water's edge.

As you read about ways to utilize your creativity, I hope you are not thinking of reasons why you can't express your creativity. You wouldn't be the only one. Here's a list of responses from people who were asked whether they take the time to express their creativity.

I'm too busy.
I don't have the money.
I have to work.
I'm not talented at anything.
I'm not the creative type.
I don't want to look foolish.
I've got to be the grown-up in the family.
I used up all my ideas.
I will, when I get through this divorce (or other distraction or obligation such as weddings, moves, term papers, work deadlines, etc.).
I'm creatively blocked.

If you have devised a rationale about why you can't express your creativity, say it aloud. And then picture yourself back in the Garden of Eden. Remember to leave your defenses at the gate. As you stroll past meadows and flowering trees, listen to God's voice: " 'See, I have given you every plant yielding seed that is upon the face of all the earth, and every tree with seed in its fruit; you shall have them for food. And to every beast of the earth, and to every bird of the air, and to everything that creeps on the earth, everything that has the breath of life, I have given every green plant for food.' And it was so" (Genesis 1:29–30).

It's true that you may be in the middle of a busy city or squeezed into a subway car, or in any number of scenarios that seem far from the Garden of Eden, but none of that negates God's offer. Your imagination, your ability to read these words and picture that beautiful scene, means that your creativity, God's spirit, His breath of life, resides within you.

That variety of life in the garden, that creative force infusing every leaf and animal represents the multiplicity of creative possibilities in your life. There is endless abundance in that garden—not just one green, but hundreds of shades and hundreds of hues of green—all reminders that contained within you is God's creative spirit, more than enough to power hundreds and hundreds of projects.

Standing right there in the middle of the garden, what happens when you try to repeat your excuse out loud? Maybe you want to say, "I'm not talented," but the droning of the bees making honey seems to drown out your words. Perhaps you're saying that you don't have the time, but there's a big inviting rock by the water and you can't resist sitting down and relaxing your mind and body. Your excuse doesn't work in here, does it? Denying your creativity is like turning your back on God's generosity. Do you see now how infinite possibilities can be born of faith?

If you can't imagine something creative that you'd be good at, don't be hard on yourself. But do take out your journal and write about experiences that stifled your creativity. Mark, a pastor from Oregon, recalled just how much he loved drawing when he was a child, and how that was stifled when his third-grade art teacher gave him a D on one project and an F for a crayon drawing. For decades afterward, he refused to draw even a doodle, and as an adult he insisted that his duties as a minister kept him too busy for "such nonsense." His wife encouraged him to start drawing again when their children were very young by giving him and their toddler a set of crayons and a coloring book. It took a while before he stopped worrying about whether he was "coloring outside the lines," but Mark eventually began enjoying the art time he shared with his daughter. As a matter of fact, his daughter has grown up to be a wonderful artist and Mark hasn't given up on his artistic bent. Last year he crafted a beautiful table for his wife, and in the fall he plans to design and build a loft bed with his daughter.

Mark's reluctance to engage in any creative endeavors stemmed directly from his childhood shaming experience. There is no greater barrier to creative energy than shame, and, happily, the opposite is also true. If we can move past shaming experiences—identifying them and telling others about them—our creativity will flow. Following are some suggestions for maximizing your creative energy.

- Prayer. Thank God for the abundance of His creation and ask Him to allow you to give back by identifying a talent and using it to the greater good or to earn a living.
- Self-encouragement. Use your nurturing inner voice to try various creative endeavors until you find one that you

LIVE LIKE YOU'RE BLESSED

literally feel you can't live without. Speak sweetly to yourself and avoid negatives, such as, "You could have done better." Instead try something along the order of, "Good for you for trying. You are so courageous."

- Sign up for a class. I've recently registered for a drama course. Acting and producing were my loves and I'm determined to keep my life in balance by paying attention to that aspect of my personality. What did you used to enjoy doing? Go for it.

- Visit a museum off the beaten track. If you live near a large city or university town, read up on unusual exhibits and museums until you find something that strikes your fancy. That doll museum in the next town or rose garden might be just what your soul is craving.

- Jot down these words from Genesis. Write the words, "And they were not ashamed" on a slip of paper and repeat them to yourself when you take a creative plunge. These words will help you remember the importance of nurturing that innocent, trusting child within you—that's where your creativity lies.

- Read *The Artist's Way: A Spiritual Path to Higher Creativity.* This workbook by Julia Cameron sets the gold standard for books that help you become more creative in any enterprise. After working through the book, you may want to start an Artist's Way group, with members supporting one another in various endeavors.

PART V

B
L
E
S **Success**
E
D

CHAPTER 13

Discerning the Path to Success

Something tells me that a number of readers who've worked their way through to this second *S* for success, in "blessed," will be disappointed by this chapter. But I pray that you'll keep reading as you learn an essential truth about my spiritual leadership: Unlike many in my profession, I don't equate faith with financial success.

I feel the need to state this since there are ministers seen on national television each week who point to their mansions, fashionable clothing, and even their jets and yachts as if suggesting that their flamboyant lifestyles were provided by God because of their devotion to Him.

I often find myself mentally wrestling with their messages, wondering, if what they claim is true, how these ministers explain poor people. Are they actually suggesting that some folks aren't rich because they don't know how to relate to God? That, of course, would be impossible to swallow, since our faith is based on Jesus Christ our Lord and Savior, who as the King of Kings might have worn silk robes and jeweled crowns, but who instead lived the modest and simple life of the son of a carpenter and as a Palestinian, a people oppressed under the Roman system.

I'm not condemning financial wealth. An ample supply of money can assist us in living blessed lives. My complaints are with those who extol unlimited earnings. Keep in mind that the *B* in "blessed" is for balance. You've heard the expression "Too much of a good thing." Well, an unlimited quest for money can throw life out of balance. God wants us to love Him and one another, and we're counseled to keep our "lives free from the love of money" (Hebrews 13:5). The fate of those who fall in love with money is exemplified by people who dominate the headlines with scandals, because they are willing to do whatever it takes to grow rich beyond measure. They're proof that life on a material plane is uneven.

To me, success means living in alignment with my deepest convictions and values. No bank can take away those assets, because my head cashier is the Holy Ghost and my deposits are acts of obedience to His will. It's the least I can do, and it's what He expects of me. Paul wrote in Philippians 2:13, "For it is God who is at work in you, enabling you, both to will and to work for His good pleasure." That message suggests that if we cooperate with divine purposes, God will work through us to accomplish His will.

The retired New Testament professor William J. Richardson, Ph.D., illustrates the working relationship that God offers by describing three fathers who are teaching their sons how to ride a two-wheeler across a street to reach home: "The first father, doubting his son's ability, keeps a steady grip on the bike as the boy pedals across," Dr. Richardson says. "The second dad is lackadaisical, leaning against a fence and watching as the boy pedals unsteadily across the street. The third father is God. As the boy takes off, He runs beside him saying, 'I won't hold on, but I'll be right beside you to offer assistance when you need me.' "

If that was one of my sons, I'd certainly want him to travel with the Lord's guidance. I'd tell my sons that if they're aiming for success, they can tap into God's wisdom by learning spiritual discernment, the spiritual way to make decisions. Spiritual discernment is a process in which we ask the Holy Spirit to lead or give direction in our lives, as we practice hearing, seeing, or feeling God's answer.

Since the onus is on us to receive the information, some people might view discernment as a test. According to this misplaced logic, if we experience failure then that means we didn't work hard enough to understand God's message, or we must be bad Christians for not following His advice. Let me assure you that God would never set us up like that. There are no hard and fast rights and wrongs in the discernment process. Sometimes the decisions we make after a long and prayerful period lead us to hard times. The way I see it, that means we're in the middle of a situation that offers an opportunity to acquire wisdom.

You know what wisdom is, don't you? Some people are confused by the word. We live at a time when many folks understandably feel compelled to get as much education as possible, perhaps earning several degrees or enrolling in one training program after another. If they work hard they might graduate with a great deal of knowledge, and I salute their efforts. Knowledge is the kind of power that can help us advance at a swifter rate on the road to success. As helpful as knowledge may be, though, it would be a mistake to confuse it with wisdom. I agree wholeheartedly with the pundit who said, "Knowledge can help you make a living; wisdom can help you make a life."

While knowledge can be gained from attending schools and reading books, wisdom comes from God. James wrote, "But if any of you lacks wisdom, let him ask of God, who gives to all generously and without reproach, and it will be given to him" (James 1:5). Did you hear that one? It's the deal of a lifetime, and let me explain why. Day after day you can turn on the television and hear cell phone companies offer free long distance service. Many of us are hesitant to sign up because we know there are hidden charges and that by the end of the month we'll end up owing more than we can afford. But think of our loving Father in Heaven, who is always willing to offer guidance. I call that long distance without hidden charges. His service is not only free but highly reliable. With God, we don't have to ask, "Can you hear me?" We know He can. Can I get a witness!

I don't want to make the process of discernment sound easy. Since we're only human, it's easy to misunderstand God's will. I'm thinking here of people like the young woman who assured me that God had sent her a sign she was marrying the right man, because after weeks of rain, the sun shone on her wedding day. A lot of people mistake acts of providence for God's answers. They might get a raise, win the lottery, marry the right guy, and think, "God's telling me I'm on the right track." Unfortunately, discerning God's will isn't like following the easy-to-read signs posted along a highway.

One helpful way to understand what God wants is to read the Bible and attend a church where you can be enlightened about scripture. Knowledge of scripture is certainly helpful when it comes to making a choice. You might be lonely, for instance, when a handsome and charming man enters your life and courts you until you fall in love with him. But later, when you discover he's married, your choice might seem pretty clear. Although he may beg you to remain with him in an adulterous relationship, you recall that adultery is the subject of the Seventh Commandment (Exodus 20:14) and you remember another passage that instructs that "marriage is honorable in all, and the bed undefiled; but fornicators and adulterers God will judge" (Hebrews 13:4). Because God gave us the gift of free will, we're sometimes caught in the struggle between right and wrong. Thanks to scripture, I've never been wishy-washy about what kind of behavior I'd expect from myself. By my standard of success—to live in alignment with my deepest convictions and values—adultery would make me feel like a failure.

As I have said, however, God's will is not always clearly discernible, but there are others who seem to keep up a running conversation with God. I'm thinking now about Bonnie Guiton Hill, Ed.D., who, at sixty-three, is one of the most notable women in America. She is a former assistant education secretary under President Ronald Reagan, served as consumer advisor to the first President Bush, was dean at the University of Virginia's McIntire School of Commerce, was president and chief executive officer of the Times Mirror Foundation, and was senior vice president of communications and public affairs for the *Los Angeles Times*. Dr. Hill is currently president of B. Hill Enterprises LLC, a consulting firm, sits on several prominent corporate boards, and is cofounder, with her husband, Walter Hill, of Icon Blue, a brand marketing firm that serves major corporations such as Honda, Toyota, and the Hilton Hotels.

This highly accomplished woman doesn't define her success by her career highlights. She is proud to say that she has a strong relationship with the Almighty and that she regularly turns to Him for guidance. She's also happily married to a man of faith, serves those who are less fortunate, enjoys loving relationships with her daughter, stepdaughters, and grandchildren, and could fill a room with people who count her as a trusted and loyal friend.

Dr. Hill's road to success wasn't paved with smooth stones, but thanks to the influence of her maternal grandmother, who was with her during much of her early childhood in Springfield, Illinois, Dr. Hill learned early on to trust God. "My grandmother gave me my spiritual foundation. She took me to church, and I can remember that when I had the chicken pox, she read the Bible aloud and talked to me about God."

Sometimes her faith seemed to compound the difficulties of her life. She didn't grow up with her biological father in the house, and she was raised hearing the details of his one and only visit to see her. Although she doesn't remember all the details of this particular event, she says, "I was about two or three and since I was preparing to eat, I began saying my blessings. My father apparently grabbed a butcher knife, stuck it in the table and told me not to say prayers with my mother." Dr. Hill would never get a chance to ask him about his actions. "When I was seven, he was stabbed and killed by one of his girlfriends."

Despite difficult circumstances, little Bonnie—the future Dr. Hill—learned to present a positive face to the world. Her mother was an alcoholic, and Bonnie learned early on to think of her as two women. "When Mom was inebriated, she was not herself. She could curse like a sailor, but somehow she always made it home. Then there was the other mom, who was sober and worked as a domestic."

Her mother's rich, white employers marveled at little Bonnie's manners, and often gave her hand-me-down clothes and shoes. To this day, Dr. Hill has trouble with her feet from those days of walking in ill-fitting shoes. Despite this and other difficulties, she has warm memories of growing up with the sober side of her mother. "She taught me to take pride in myself. And she was so proper that she wouldn't take the garbage out without taking the rollers out of her hair. Her motto was that even if you're dressed in rags, they should be clean and your hair should be neat and your shoes shined."

People familiar with Dr. Hill know that this maternal message stuck with her. She is known for her elegant appearance. One of her longtime friends swears that she saw her at an indoor parking lot, and that although the wind outside was whipping umbrellas from pedestrians' hands, Dr. Hill glided inside on designer heels, carrying a beautiful umbrella matching a raincoat that fit her slender frame like the proverbial glove. "And not a hair on her well-groomed head was out of place," the friend adds.

Long before she grew into that perfectly coiffed businesswoman, she was little Bonnie with hell to pay. Her mother continued to attract violent men, and as a result, "She was a battered woman," Dr. Hill recalls. "One night when I was ten, I was sitting on the stairs of our house. Mom wasn't home, but somehow I knew that wherever she was she was being beaten. I started praying to God, asking for His protection and asking what I could do to protect her. As I watched the moon, a dove flew out of the clouds and landed on my shoulder." Dr. Hill says the bird felt real to her.

A dove is generally a sign of peace, but the evening did not prove to be tranquil. Shortly afterward, Bonnie's mother and stepfather returned from their evening out. "Mom was black and blue from an-other beating." Little Bonnie decided to take matters into her own hands. "After they fell asleep, I got a butcher knife from the kitchen and stood over my mother's husband." The intoxicated adults were sleeping deeply, but, as if sensing that his life was in peril, the man's eyes flew open. "He saw me, and he started screaming and woke my mother."

That next morning, when her stepfather left for work, little Bon-nie, as if interpreting the dove as a message to "fly away," packed her clothes and her mother's and, grasping the money she'd saved from a small allowance, convinced her mother to flee with her. They took a train to a nearby town and lived for a short while with her father's mother, before eventually moving to Milwaukee, then to Oakland, California.

Without family to lend emotional support, Dr. Hill's mother in-creasingly depended on alcohol. "She stopped working and went on welfare. It was humiliating. Social workers would go through my closets, checking to see whether my mother had any men hiding in there." Dr. Hill had arrived in Oakland in time to start the seventh grade. "It seemed a lot of the kids knew who was on welfare and they teased me about it." Her clothes may have helped give away her situation. A preteen by then, Dr. Hill dressed in borrowed clothes, and the outfits were often too large for her slender frame.

With all these difficulties, she didn't excel in school, although some teachers thought she could. "One of the teachers saw I was ac-ademically advanced and offered to promote me, but Mom wanted me to stay with my age group. I was so bored in class that I started sleeping." By her junior year of high school she'd fallen behind her classmates. "Two teachers pulled me aside and said, 'We know you're

better than Ds and Fs.' I told them that I didn't have an appreciation for Socrates and Plato, because I wanted to develop a skill that
would help me land a job, so Mom and I could get off welfare.
They enrolled me in a vocational course." She proceeded to learn
secretarial skills, and after graduation passed a civil service exam.
With her first paycheck from her clerk's job, Dr. Hill moved herself
and her mother off welfare.

Dr. Hill's life only looked easy from the outside. She'd been attending a local church for several years, and from the time she was
fifteen, the pastor had been sexually abusing her. "I was a very young
teenager, not worldly at all. And he said that if I told anyone, he
could make my mother die. I believed him because I'd seen him heal
people, and he had a way of pointing out his enemies to me. When
any of those people happened to get sick or die or some tragedy be-
fell them, this reverend claimed it happened because of his power. I
was terrified of him. I never told anyone what he was doing to me,
and I kept it a secret. It lasted for four years." Money from her new
job gave her a little leverage. When Dr. Hill was nineteen, she moved
away in the middle of the night, insisting that her mother not pass
on her new address if the minister sought her out.

Her relationship with this minister didn't destroy her faith.
"Thank God, I could see that there were other good people in the
church. But I did learn a year later that he'd also been abusing another girl." The full impact of this minister's harm didn't quite reg-
ister, until after Dr. Hill's first marriage, at twenty-four.

She and her husband, Harvey Guiton, an Oakland businessman,
tried to conceive a child, but a doctor explained that this would be
impossible. "He told me that I had a displaced uterus. I knew how
that had happened. When I was still very young and this minister

was abusing me, I missed my period and he was so terrified that I was pregnant and people would discover what he was doing that he paid a dentist to perform a C-section on me. The procedure was brutal, and it turned out that I wasn't even pregnant."

Years later, the doctor's advice to the contrary, Dr. Hill and her husband did conceive, and she gave birth to a beautiful baby son. Unfortunately, the infant lived only four days, due to birth complications connected to her uterine difficulties. This time the doctor was certain that Dr. Hill would never conceive again.

Through prayer and meditation, she emerged from the situation knowing just what she should do. "I went back to my old pastor and told him I'd lost my son, due to complications he'd caused. I said that I'd never forget what he'd done, but that I forgave him. With God's help, I knew that I would never be all right if I didn't let my anger go. When I forgave that man, the weight of the world seemed to drop off of me." Two weeks later, she and her husband had conceived again, and this child lived. Nichele, now a college graduate, a business executive, and a wife and mother of two, lives within driving distance of Dr. Hill's home in southern California.

Over the years, Dr. Hill has continued to face her challenges by asking the Lord for guidance. Her husband, Harvey, succumbed to heart disease, but not before he saw his young wife develop into a force to be reckoned with. She eventually took classes at Mills College, where she was employed as a secretary, and in the evenings attended two different community colleges. In two and a half years, she earned a bachelor of science degree, majoring in psychology, and followed that up with a master's degree in educational psychology from California State University, Hayward. Years later, she earned a doctorate in education from the University of California, Berkeley.

When questioned about how she was able to accomplish so much, Dr. Hill insists that she still prays over decisions and then listens for a still small voice. "I tell my daughter and my stepdaughters not to be afraid to ask God for a sign. When I've had job offers, I've visualized myself in the job and then prayed over it. There are quite a few things I've turned down on the basis of these responses."

One need only meet Dr. Hill to understand that one of her most persistent prayers has been answered. "I wanted God to help me move on from the old. I've prayed that I'd learn from each harsh experience but not make those experiences part of my present. You can't hold on to hostility and at the same time move on."

Her story provides answers about how the process of discernment works. Consider the quote that I mentioned earlier in this chapter: "If any of you lack wisdom, ask of God, who gives to all generously and ungrudgingly, and it will be given you" (James 1:5). Now that you're familiar with Dr. Hill's story, you may better appreciate the words that follow in the next verse. "But ask in faith, never doubting, for the one who doubts is like a wave of the sea, driven and tossed by the winds; for the do^bter, being double-minded and unstable in every way, must not expect to receive anything from the Lord" (James 1:6–8).

As you digest those words, please remember that this is not the time to blame yourself for wrong turns on your path or for moments of doubt. James 1:6–8 offers a loving promise. If you have a strong, unwavering faith in the Lord, He will guide you. Don't forget to continue thanking God for all that He has given you and for working through you in the most difficult situations. True faith requires the understanding that He loves you just as much when you're in doubt or when you're suffering so greatly that even His voice seems to be drowned out. After World War II, as more Nazi atrocities came to light, a message was found on the wall of a concentration camp: "I believe, even when He is silent." Yes, even when God seems silent, He is with you.

And be assured that as you continue to work through this book, you are demonstrating your faith in Him, not in me or my words. I believe in my deepest heart of hearts that He is blessing me by allowing me to offer you words to live by. God, I thank you God, for this opportunity, and in all ways and all things, I will remain your humble, grateful, and loyal servant.

CHAPTER 14

Finding Your Holy Mission

As we continue forging new definitions of success, while exploring the second *S* in "blessed," you may want to set aside time to compose a mission statement. Just in case you're wondering what a mission statement might be, let's look closer at that term. *Webster's Dictionary* defines "mission" as "the special duty or errand that a person or group is sent out to do." Most of us have heard of Christian missionaries who devote their lives to the mission of converting souls to Christ. And as you probably know, a statement is something that you tell or declare in a formal or definite way that serves as a record or report.

When it comes to composing your mission statement, just forget the word "formal," or even "report" for that matter, both of which make the process sound intimidating; something akin to an assignment that might be marked, corrected, and graded by a teacher. Composing your mission statement can actually turn out to be fun, and may well prove to be one of the best things you've ever done for yourself.

You probably have a hard time believing that claim if you've ever worked for a corporation or nonprofit center where there were long and exhaustive meetings, with folks debating lofty goals and insisting on including phrases that reflect their areas of expertise. Writing your personal mission statement will be more like soul work, as enjoyable as sitting around with a group of favorite friends to discuss *your* dreams and hopes and aspirations.

Simply put, a mission statement is a clearly written note—you can write it in your journal or on a separate sheet of paper—that might run anywhere from five sentences to a couple of pages, declaring your goals and objectives in life. It can begin with a vision of your future and continue by stating who you want to be. Despite its simplicity, it's absolutely necessary for those of us who hope to experience success. Because if we don't know where we're going, we might wind up taking so many detours that we never reach a meaningful destination.

Hopefully your soothing internal voice has kicked in, and if not, you may be using this as another opportunity to put yourself down. Maybe you're thinking that you've probably wasted time because you should have written a personal mission statement long ago. Let me assure you that your past experiences do count, no matter how unfocused they may seem. Your mission statement, just like this book, is all about faith, faith that God loves you and created you with a purpose. And because He brings all things to completion, you can trust that no matter what your past may include or what is occurring now, all will be well and will work for the good.

I certainly traveled alternate routes in my lifetime. After my post-graduation experience in Ghana, I returned to Africa a few years later, backpacking through the continent with Yolanda King, the daughter of Dr. Martin Luther King, Jr. She and I had not known one another until we embarked on our journey. Mutual friends had set up the introduction for the purpose of the trip. Yolanda and I only had a few hours together before our departure from New York's Kennedy Airport, but we bonded during our trip.

As for my career, I wasn't quite sure which direction to take. At nineteen, after earning a bachelor's degree at Emerson College, majoring in mass communications and speech with a minor in theater, I applied at my home church for a license to preach. While waiting for a date for my first sermon, with my mother's urging, I applied and was accepted at the Teachers College of Columbia University to study education technology. Between classes, I traveled to various states and performed with *Voices Incorporated: Journey to Blackness*, taking theater into classrooms and teaching through drama. Two years later, armed with a master of arts and teaching experience, I was prepared for a career in the educational field, but I moved in a different direction.

Relocating to the nation's capital, I lived with my Aunt Katherine—one of the nieces my dad had helped raise—while I trained to be a producer at WJLA-TV. At the end of the training program, I accepted a job with the station as a floor manager and was quickly promoted up the ladder to assistant producer. But something was interfering with my peace of mind, and I believe it was God's call. Despite opportunities for advancement in the broadcasting field, I was growing convinced that God wanted me to step from behind the scene into the somewhat uncomfortable preaching limelight. Keep in mind that in the late seventies, women preachers were an even rarer breed than they are today.

Testing the waters, I enrolled in night classes at Howard University's seminary, but my television career was taking off, and I joined the staffs at WBZ-TV in Boston, and then WPLG in Miami. My salary more than doubled during those five years, but the Lord seemed to be guiding me back home to New York.

I sent out a few feelers, and job opportunities in the Big Apple began to present themselves, including one possibility with the CBS news program *Sixty Minutes* and another with ABC's *Good Morning America*. Strangely enough, I grew interested in a public relations position at Bronx Lebanon Hospital.

When people asked me why I left the lucrative and exciting broadcast industry, I could only explain that I was following a call. I'm also a strong believer in the notion that to everything there is a season. With God's guidance we know when a season is over. That doesn't necessarily mean, though, that we always take His blessed advice. God may be saying one thing, while your mind suggests another course of action and your heart says something completely different. In my case, my best friends in the world live in Washington, D.C. To this day, I still take the train to Union Station so we can meet for laugh-filled, intimate lunches. Although my heart was telling me to move to D.C., no job presented itself in that area during this time in my life.

The hospital job in New York was still available, and I accepted. The salary and benefits were good, but more importantly, I wouldn't be required to work the crazy schedule often expected of a television producer. I believe God was getting me positioned in just the right place, at the right time. Not long after returning to New York, I applied for and was accepted at Union Theological Seminary and attended classes during my lunch hours and after work. Even with a more moderate work schedule, though, I often found myself torn between my duties to work and school.

The turning point in my career occurred on one particularly high-stress day, when I'd rushed from an exam given by the Reverend Doctor James Forbes. Union Seminary has a plethora of gifted teachers, but even among these illustrious scholars, Dr. Forbes is a standout. In 1989, he was installed as the senior pastor of Manhattan's Riverside Church, with its international, interracial, interdenominational congregation of 2,400. Often called the "preacher of preachers," Reverend Forbes was named by *Ebony* magazine as one of America's greatest black preachers and recognized by *Newsweek* as one of the most effective preachers in the English language. This gifted man was my preaching teacher. I'd rushed from his final exam, trying to get to Bronx Lebanon Hospital, where a major news event was unfolding. As the head of publicity, I was expected to address journalists.

Wouldn't you know then that I'd get caught in a major traffic jam just as I was driving across the 155th Street Bridge? Sitting there with my stomach in knots, I felt I was letting everyone down, including myself. I finally looked skyward and said, "God, I can't do this anymore. I'm going to devote my life to preaching your word." No sooner had the words departed from my lips than the traffic opened up, like the Red Sea. As soon as possible, I phoned the hospital and explained that they wouldn't see me that afternoon, and then I went back to my exam. That evening, I turned in my resignation at the hospital. I've never looked back. A month from the day I made the decision, Pastor Wells phoned and told me it was time to be ordained.

My first opportunity to serve as a pastor was a tough inner-city assignment, Mariners' Temple, a predominantly black parish on

Manhattan's Lower East Side, in the heart of Chinatown. I made it a point to keep the conversation going with God as I introduced myself to the fifteen senior citizens who made up the congregation. Over the course of several months, with God's guidance, membership at Mariners' grew to 150 souls. Most were struggling members of the working poor or people barely getting by on welfare, and they had numerous problems that required a pastor's support. I was twenty-three and single, and I gave them everything I had, putting in long days—an effort of 200 percent.

But there's a cost for moving at a frantic pace without direction. After seven years I was totally burned out. A year earlier, I'd met the dean of Harvard's Divinity School, so when he called in August 1990, to offer me a Presidential Administration Fellowship, I wanted to accept, but I worried that my parishioners might not agree to me taking a year's leave from work. Calling a congregational meeting, I addressed a hushed room and was soon surprised by the response of my parishioners. People stood up and applauded. They'd assumed I'd called them together to quit and seemed genuinely happy to learn that I only wanted to be away a year.

The only difficulty I encountered from that point was from other pastors, warning that if I left the church under interim leadership, I wouldn't have a congregation to return to. Black churches didn't have a tradition of their pastors taking time off. As it turned out, my leave set up a paradigm for black churches allowing their pastors to take sabbaticals.

My time at Harvard was undoubtedly a gift from God. The college is like a little city, with every resource imaginable. Thanks to the fellowship, I was given money, enjoyed the benefits of an officer of Harvard, and was housed in a charming apartment on the Charles

River. Mom was with me when I first entered the campus. We were mindful that our ancestors had picked cotton, and it was like an out-of-body experience for both of us.

The Harvard program allowed me to set my schedule, and many times I sat by the Charles River, feeling gratitude at the deepest and most immediate level. The experience was beautiful and spiritual, but religious reflection without a connection to real life is like a carefully preserved house of cards: If the two are disconnected, sooner or later, a difficult moment or question will expose its fragile or tentative state. Not all of us can stop and sit by a river to ponder the direction that we dream of taking, but I urge you to take a weekend, day, or an afternoon to engage in the discernment process and, with God's guidance, write about your future.

You might begin by writing a letter to God. I did, expressing my hopes and dreams for the next decade, intentionally omitting goals that weren't in keeping with His plans for me. At first it was difficult to think purely of my dreams, because I'd spent the last several years focused on the needs of my parishioners. After awhile though, the ideas began to flow. I wanted to find a venue for spreading the good news of the gospel to a larger audience. And because I had spent time in schools, working with the poor and disenfranchised, I added that I wanted to use my convictions to shape national policy decisions. On a more personal level, I hoped to fall and love and be loved, and to start a family, instilling in my children the values that had been passed on to me. I described a home filled with love and laughter, and above all, obedience to God. There was one specific feature I wanted concerning our home: that it be located near a body of water, where I could feel my soul restored.

I'd written down my objectives, and now another and important aspect of this work was figuring out how I could achieve the desired results. I realized then that I needed to return to school and begin working on a doctoral degree. As the first female American Baptist pastor, I had to be as prepared as possible. As for the marriage prospects, I promised myself that I'd give it awhile and then begin a conversation with God on that very subject.

After describing my personal vision and making some practical decisions, I continued through prayer and through discernment to seek God's advice about my mission in life. I heard the Lord through the voice of Isaiah: "Learn to do good, seek justice, rescue the oppressed, defend the orphans; plead for the windows." For someone weary at the soul, the idea of finding relief for the oppressed seemed monumental. The more I thought about it, though, the clearer the vision grew of me speaking out on behalf of those who could not speak for themselves. The widows and orphans of biblical days could easily be viewed as my congregants at Missionary Baptist, as well as people of every race and socio-economic background who desired fuller lives in Christ. This renewed my determination to return to my parish and inspire my congregants to improve their lives.

I also began writing my third book, *Too Blessed to Be Stressed: Words of Wisdom for Women on the Move,* offering advice on recovering from burnout. The book was widely received and helped me find that larger audience I'd written about in my vision. My first two books, *Wise Women Bearing Gifts: Joys and Struggles of Their Faith* and *Sister to Sister: Devotions for and from African American Women,* had been published by a small press.

Once the sabbatical ended, I joyfully returned to Mariners' Temple, where I stayed for five more years. In that time I commuted to Dayton, Ohio, where I earned my doctorate of ministry at the

United Theological Seminary. A few years later, I met and married my wonderful husband.

Although there were pitstops and detours along the way, my vision for my life continued to unfold much in the way that I had hoped. But let's face it; life often occurs in overdrive. In 1991, I resigned from my job with the full intention of devoting time to starting and raising the family I'd described in my mission vision. The year before, I'd applied for a White House fellowship—remember that dream that called for influencing public policy on a national level—and as life would have it, both the fellowship and the baby arrived at virtually the same time. I'd applied with slim hopes. After all, two thousand people applied for this yearlong paid fellowship, which allowed winners to work in the offices of the president, vice president, or a cabinet member. I was accepted in July of 1993, and was expected to report at the White House by September.

Ron encouraged me to accept the fellowship, even though he thought it best to remain at his Manhattan job. I took off for the capital with our infant Samuel, and initially felt discouraged when I couldn't locate a suitable nursery for him. But persistence paid off. I called the White House program for kids a second time and learned that a slot had miraculously opened up.

Securing a position at the White House didn't go as smoothly. No one seemed to have an idea about how they could use my skills, and I was required to interview at different offices, hoping someone would offer me a job. In the last few months, I'd immersed myself in policy issues, preparing myself for the tough issues I thought might be pertinent to President Clinton's welfare reform. To my surprise, none of the people interviewing me asked me about policy; they wanted to know about my ministry. At that point, the only real hitch as I saw it was that my potential employers would expect me to work long days, without regard to my baby's needs.

I should have relaxed and reminded myself that God always prepares a way. In one interview, one of my sweet little baby's photos caught the eye of Carol H. Rasco, White House Advisor for Domestic Policy. Rasco, a mother of two, is a former middle school counselor, volunteer, disability advocate, and policy counselor at the state and national level. To say we have many interests in common is an understatement.

Carol Rasco looked at Samuel's photo and said, "You're going to have offers to work in various departments, but keep in mind that the most important thing for you to do is pick up your baby every day at five." Before the day ended, I had seven job offers, including the Domestic Policy Council, headed by Carol Rasco. I accepted her offer and became her domestic policy analyst. Her office oversaw all of the issues related to children and family. The knowledge I'd accumulated in teachers' college and as a classroom drama teacher added to my value as an analyst—so that "detour" in my life had not been a wasted effort.

During the year I worked at the White House, President Clinton spoke at many churches. It wasn't long before his speechwriter was sending the president's speeches over to me, asking for feedback. After a while, the president began to see me and began referring to me as "the Baptist preacher from the Bronx." At times the two of us would walk down the hall together discussing various issues. On a few occasions he stopped at my office, stuck his head through the doorway, and asked, "May I come in for a minute?" I could see Secret Service agents gathering outside as he entered.

Looking back, I realize that this was the point at which I became convinced that God not only opens doors for us, He also helps us step through the doorway. That means that no matter how detailed our mission statement might be, He's likely to give us far more than we asked for. I was blessed by the unfolding opportunities around me. Sometimes during that year at the White House it was difficult to imagine that what I was experiencing was real. And there was Ron, offering encouraging words over the phone most weeknights and in person on Friday nights and Saturdays, when he joined me and our first son in D.C.

There's another lesson here: When you visualize your future, don't be ashamed to tell God what you truly want. It's not as if you want Him to wave a magic wand and deliver the goods. You'll recall that I asked for a home by the water. My family and I have one, but that doesn't mean we don't have to work hard to pay the mortgage.

I hope you've learned from my story that no matter where you might be at this time in your life—a young student, middle-aged career person, parent with young children, minister leading a large urban parish, just getting off of welfare—it doesn't matter. From the vantage point of writing your mission, it's as if your life will start from this day forward. If that sounds like a line from a marriage ceremony, that's not surprising: A personal mission statement merges the person you are today with the person you want to become. Here are some pointers on shaping your mission statement. As you read through them, you might want to jot down ideas in your journal.

- Make it holy. Use the letters BLESSED to remind yourself of what you want your life to be like. Remember that *B* is for balance. Ask yourself how you might achieve a balance among your work, spiritual, and personal needs. The *L* for love is also important to factor into your dream. God, who is love, wants us to have love in our lives. And you'll also need the energy in *E* for a healthy emotional state; the *S*, which is, of course, the Lord's Holy Spirit, and another *S* for success at realizing your dreams. In upcoming chapters, we'll explore the second *E* for encouragement and *D*, offering suggestions on becoming even more devoted to the Lord. Visualize it all, asking God to guide your way.

• Stress the positive. You certainly know who you don't want to be. When Lee was asked about how she saw herself in the future, she said she didn't want to become someone who stopped growing. When asked to turn that around into a positive statement, she realized that she wanted to spend a lot of time traveling after her retirement, learning about new cultures. She also realized that she wants to learn how to swim. Ask yourself what you want to be like.

• Recognize your gifts. You've worked through "blessed" sufficiently to no longer feel the need to "hide your light under a bushel." By now you may have recognized and thanked God for your special gifts. These may range from being welcoming to strangers or being good with kids to being a good public speaker or artist or singer. Ask yourself which of these gifts you'd like to continue developing and consider how you might use them to accomplish your mission, and perhaps, to earn additional income, if necessary.

• Picture someone you love and/or admire. Some people mention celebrities with admirable traits, such as Maya

Angelou, who always seems to speak with authority and wisdom, because they want to emulate these individuals. Others mention a favorite aunt or recall a parent who was especially generous. Ask yourself what characteristics you'd like to be remembered for by loved ones.

• Give it a timeline. When you write your mission and visualize your future, give yourself from two to five years for events to unfold. Check with your vision every six months to ensure that you don't stray too far from your chosen path.

• Don't get too serious. Remember that this is not a contract that someone will sue you over if you don't live up to your end of the agreement. These statements are more like welcoming signs posted on the boundaries of your new neighborhood. That's the tone you'd like to establish: "Hi. We're so glad you're here. You're just the sort of person we've been waiting for, someone who is _____." Fill in the characteristics you hope to develop.

• Use quotes. I remind myself of who I want to become by carrying around a small notebook filled with quotations from people I admire. During difficult moments, these quotations help me remain focused on my dreams.

CHAPTER 15

Creating Financial Health and Wealth

The young parishioners were working hard to hold it to-gether. After ten years of marriage, Sean and Louisa were going through a crisis. Sean, a forty-one-year-old shipping clerk, had applied for a credit card and was shocked when the company denied his application, citing a poor credit record. "I thought we had a great credit rating," he told me. Since Louisa hadn't been home to offer an explanation, Sean searched through their monthly statements and discovered a secret that seemed powerful enough to tear them apart: "We're $37,000 in debt," Sean said angrily, and he slipped a stack of frayed envelopes onto my desk. "Louisa has been lying to me all this time."

Louisa, thirty-six, who manages a law office, balled up a tissue and swiped at her tears. "I haven't been lying, Reverend Cook." She gave her husband a sorrowful look. "Baby, me not telling you about those debts was my way of protecting you. It's not like I went out and bought clothes or new shoes with that money. The two of us don't earn enough to pay our bills. When I started getting those blank checks in the mail they seemed like money from heaven. I used it for the kids' school fees . . . that time my mother got sick, car repairs, and that time when we needed the work on the roof . . . those kind of things." When her husband refused to make eye contact with her, she shrugged and turned back toward me. "I got behind in the payments, and I didn't want Sean staying awake nights, like me, worrying every time the phone rang, thinking it's gonna be a collection agency. I've been through hell worrying."

It would be difficult to find a pastor that hasn't encountered a similar scene with parishioners stressed out over bills and desperate to find a way out of their financial entanglements. Like Sean and Louisa, many are hardworking people who have had to put their dreams of success on hold simply to pay attention to the details of surviving. It's no secret that it's harder to get ahead than ever before, what with high prices on basics such as medicine and housing and the soaring gasoline prices, and companies cutting back on employee health care and retirement benefits. As a result, increasing numbers of people are caught in financial binds. Throughout the years, I have talked with a number of people struggling with financial issues, and they often fall into one of several categories.

- Recent college graduates. Although saddled with educational loans, many are so relieved to have finished college that they want to start their adult lives off with a bang, and that often means a new car. But then they're faced with the heavy toll of supporting themselves, making payments on their school debts and their car, and meeting other expenses, such as the cost of building a professional wardrobe.

- Single mother. Those who can't count on generous child-support payments from former spouses are burdened by the need to pay for child care and a host of other expenses that two people should be sharing. As the sole breadwinners, they feel their finances derailed by unanticipated expenses.

- Divorced fathers. They're trying to do the right thing and support those they've left behind, plus they're trying to keep roofs over their own heads, and they too are caught in a bind.

- The working elderly. Many have retired from long-held jobs and now work one or two part-time jobs. Sometimes they're forced to choose between medicine and food, both of which they need for life.

- Couples. Sean and Louisa are typical of many families trying to live the American Dream. For too many people, the dream has become a nightmare.

- Shopaholics. They seem to get more of a thrill out of buying new clothes, shoes, or things than they do in actually wearing or using them. Many shopaholics have closets filled with clothes with tags attached to them. What's generally most surprising about people with this problem is that even when their income increases, they find a way to keep spending more than they make.

- Addicted to debt. These individuals get in the habit of handling crises by running up charges on their credit cards or cashing those blank checks that banks mail out. Like Louisa, people addicted to debt can often justify why they need the money, but the more of that seemingly "free" money that they spend, the deeper a hole they dig for themselves. After a while they may feel like modern-day sharecroppers, working solely to keep up the payments on their debts, so they just can't seem to get ahead.

The kind of money pressures these people are struggling with would appear to be beyond the realm of my spiritual guidance. And while it's true that I do often recommend seeking expert advice, I couldn't possibly turn away folks like Sean and Louisa who are in desperate need of shoring up their spiritual resources. Yes, money problems absolutely impinge upon spiritual issues.

After all, money represents a portion of our time, talent, and energy in a form that can be negotiated. The Divine doesn't expect us to simply be good stewards over our tithed portion of income. He wants us to honor the other 90 percent of what we earn. Since our time, talent, and energy come from God, we honor Him by demonstrating good stewardship over all our gifts. Underscoring that point, Obie McKenzie, a managing director for Merrill Lynch, who also leads a Bible study group at Manhattan's Canaan Baptist Church of Christ, refers to I Corinthians 10:26: "For the earth is the Lord's, and the fullness thereof." McKenzie says, "The earth and everything on it belongs to the Lord. We come into the world naked and we will leave naked. We're just here on a lease plan. God gives us the authority to utilize his resources and expects us to use them to help others. If we don't obey, we'll derive no satisfaction from our money."

That being the case, why should we use our God-given talents to fill the coffers of a credit card company? Wouldn't we be far better off if we followed God's word and used our money to help those individuals who could really use our help? And that brings me to another point about the nexus of money and the spirit. Financial troubles can keep us from fulfilling our holy mission in life. Louisa, for example, who believes her life's mission is to help educate young people, was studying to become an elementary school teacher. But her desperate financial straits derailed her plans when she had to stop taking classes at a local college.

Financial problems also press down on our emotional energy, which can keep us from feeling and living as if we're blessed. As discussed earlier, we need to be able to draw from our emotional reserve to be at our best, whether we're launching or maintaining a new creative endeavor or relationship. One self-employed woman whose house was in foreclosure was surprised at how quickly she was able to start generating more cash once she took action to shore up her finances. Robbing Peter to pay Paul is emotionally exhausting.

Failed finances can also distance us from our inner spirit. As we are asked in Isaiah 55:2, "Why do you spend your money for that which is not bread and your labor for that which does not satisfy?" The question posited is a good one: Why spend money on that which has no intrinsic value? So what about that new designer bag that you may have charged on your credit card or that unplanned trip to the islands? While creating a momentary thrill, what do they mean for you in the long run? Don't misunderstand me. I enjoy spontaneity and certainly have an appreciation for the perfect pair of heels, but not at the cost of throwing my finances out of whack. Besides, even the hottest pair of heels can't fill my spiritual hunger. What I need is available for the asking. It was Jesus who told us, "I am the bread of life" (John 6:48).

And let's not forget the subject of success, in this final exploration of the second *S* in "blessed." In today's computer age, taking a look at someone's credit record is as easy as a potential employer pushing a few buttons. A poor credit history can leave you stuck in the slow track, far away from the mission you've discerned with God's help.

Financial recovery expert Glinda Bridgforth counseled one woman who left her high-level management job in the human resources department of an insurance company. This woman was humiliated when a head hunter confided that the reason she wasn't getting many job offers was that corporations were frightened off when they saw she was late in paying some of her bills. Bridgforth says, "It's no longer unusual for companies to use your credit rating as a criterion for judging you when you're applying for a job." She points out that a poor credit score can also translate into paying higher interest rates on a mortgage, which will leave you with a lot less money for doing the right thing. It might also mean being denied that apartment you want to rent, which can certainly dim your sense of abundance.

The point is, even if you aren't in a financial hole, if you're not where you want to be, start now to work toward financial health. And set an ultimate goal of creating wealth. Notice I didn't suggest that you should aim to grow rich. "Rich" pertains solely to money. As financial wizard and Bible teacher Obie McKenzie reminds us: "Wealth is not measured by how much you have but how little you need. Wealth is rooted in contentment and satisfaction. A real sense of abundance is created by the gift of presence; the ability to stay in the moment, not in the past or in the future."

That may sound like a strange mouthful coming from a man whose job requires him to put together pools of money, as in a recent $4-billion investment deal. But McKenzie says his spiritual roots help him see beyond that which money can buy. "The Christian faith is grounded in the word 'giving,' as in God *gave* his only begotten son." McKenzie says that we don't need to be rich to give, not if we follow his golden monetary rules: Don't borrow money (unless it's for something like buying property); get rid of credit card debt, which can be ruinous; and don't spend more than you have.

Glinda Bridgforth agrees, and offers another word of advice: "Even if things seem out of control, take action. Don't bury your head in the sand. There are steps you can take to get started on the road to financial recovery." She should know. Bridgforth, a former bank executive and author of a series of best-selling financial advice books, was mired in debt following a painful divorce. Today she has not only rebuilt her finances, but started a holistic financial management agency that counsels clients throughout the United States, and is a frequent guest on television and radio shows. Bridgforth is also a joyful newlywed. Her husband, by the way, is a good Christian man—and as far as I'm concerned, there can be no higher endorsement. Bridgforth, who took action steps to recover her finances, never faltered in her daily habit of thanking God for His gifts, and asking for His continued guidance. In fact, she readily credits God for helping to bring her right to where He wants her to be. She is indeed a woman of wealth and wisdom.

Here are some action steps to help you shore up shaky finances or save or invest more cash so you can carry out your mission in life.

Taking Charge of Your Financial Future with God's Help

I. Ask God for help. As you speak to God through prayer, continue to thank Him for showering you with gifts and for continuing to keep you strong and focused as you bring yourself to financial health and wealth.

2. Forgive yourself. If your finances are not where they need to be, take responsibility by taking action, but don't waste emotional energy blaming yourself. Corporations spend millions of dollars devising advertising campaigns that make their products and services seem irresistible, so it should not be surprising that you have been lured by their messages. Use your internalized nurturing voice to soothe and comfort yourself. Focusing on your God-given mission in life will build up your resistance.

3. Keep tithing. This may sound self-serving coming from a minister, but not if you keep in mind that you don't tithe to your pastor. You tithe to the glory of God. You tithe because you're blessed. You tithe because God wants you to. The practice of tithing dates back to the Old Testament, when those who learned of God's glory began setting aside one tenth of their earnings for God, and lived on the other 90 percent. (After you have set aside 10 percent for God, try to save the same amount for your future goals.) I can personally testify that when you honor God first, He truly blesses your life. Scripture tells us that if we tithe, the Lord will open the windows of heaven and pour down overflowing blessings on us (Malachi 3:10). In other words, God will give us more than we'd ever hoped for. If you're struggling to keep your bills paid and wondering how you can possibly pay 10 percent of your income to the church, try writing the check at the start of each month (or record the amount

on a slip of paper). During the next few weeks, thank God for money-generating ideas and revitalized energy as you go about earning the amount you have recorded. You'll get there. Giving money will boost your emotional and physical energy levels.

4. Balance your checkbook. Sure it's one of those pain-in-the-neck chores, but if you're not already doing it, this is an important first step in taking charge of your finances. Returned bank checks are costly and embarrassing. And we aren't the only ones who make accounting mistakes—bank employees do too, because they're only human. You shouldn't have to pay for their mistakes, or your own. Banks make it easy today to check your balance online, but you'll still want to balance your account at the end of each month.

5. Learn about compound interest. Remember the scenes in horror movies when someone got stuck in quicksand, and as they struggled, seemed to get pulled in deeper? The reason it's so important for you to pay off any credit card debt that you might owe is that these companies charge you compound interest. According to the Internet site moneyinstructor.com: "Compound interest means that the interest will include interest calculated on the interest." For example, if $5,000 is invested for two years and the interest rate is 10 percent compounded, at the end of the first year the interest would be $5,000 × 0.10, or $500. In the second year, the interest rate of 10 percent will be applied not only to the $5,000 but also to the $500 interest of the first

year. Thus, in the second year the interest would be $5,500 × 0.10, or $550. So pay off your credit card debts as soon as possible, doubling up payments when you can.

6. Get rid of extraneous credit cards. You can probably get by using just one for emergencies or for charges that you can afford to pay off by the end of every month. One woman I know follows up every charge by mailing a check for that amount to her credit card company. This way, she doesn't find any forgotten charges when her statement arrives. If you've abused credit cards in the past, cut up all but one and seal that one in a zip-top plastic bag and store it in your freezer. Use it only for emergencies.

7. Attend debt-elimination seminars. My church's development corporation sponsors financial literacy or debt elimination seminars, led by financial experts. Parishioners who attend and eventually pay off their debts often comment on the sense of freedom they experience at being debt-free for the first time in years. Debt is an embarrassing and oppressive force. If your church sponsors one of these seminars, I urge you to attend these goal-oriented meetings. If your church does not sponsor these seminars, organize other folks to get one started.

8. Seek outside help for debt emergencies. If you need help now and there are no debt elimination seminars being held through your church, contact the National Foundation for Credit Counseling on the Web at

www.nfcc.org, or phone the organization in Silver
Springs, Maryland, at (301) 589-5600, to locate low-
cost financial counseling in your area.

9. Slow down on ATM withdrawals. If your money is
shaky, limit yourself to one ATM withdrawal a week,
and then be sure to record all transactions in your
checkbook. Frequently withdrawing money from an
ATM adds to the illusion of picking it off trees. Before
you start spending, thank God for the money you do
have, and then list the ways you need to spend that
money. When you stick to your plan and resist impulse
buys, congratulate yourself.

10. Handle your money with care. Smooth out those dollar
bills in your wallet and arrange them by denomination—
fives with fives, tens with tens, etc. This is another way
of showing respect to that which represents your time,
talent, and energy in a negotiable form. You work hard
for your money and, from this point on, promise to treat
it and yourself with respect.

11. Substitute a spending plan for a budget. Rather than
writing an impossible-to-follow budget, record every cent
you spend for a month. This will give you an accurate
picture of what you're spending, and allow you to figure
out ways to bring in extra money, if necessary, and find
areas where you can cut costs. Glinda Bridgforth's *Money
Mastery Book*, for recording twelve months of spending,
can be ordered online at www.bridgforthfinancial.com.
Remember to celebrate your spending cuts as you trim
"fat." For example, if you spend four bucks a day on

gourmet coffee drinks, start brewing it yourself at home, or do your hair yourself between salon visits.

12. Save something. No matter how much you may have to dole out to creditors, put some aside in a savings account on a regular basis. You work hard and you deserve to pay yourself.

13. Read all about it. One of the best books that can help you is *How to Get Out of Debt, Stay Out of Debt and Live Prosperously,* by Jerrold Mundis. In addition to offering practical solutions, this book forces readers to confront their emotional money issues. Two other excellent books that also delve into the emotional realm and offer nuts and bolts advice are Bridgforth's "Girl" series—*Girl, Get Your Money Straight!* and *Girl, Get Your Credit Straight!,* which is scheduled to be published in 2007. All of Bridgforth's books can be ordered through her website, www.bridgforthfinancial.com.

14. Tear up blank checks that come in the mail. Louisa found an effective way to stop putting aside these blank checks to use on rainy days, a practice that later came back to haunt her in the form of out-of-control debts. She says, "I started picturing them as a syringe filled with drugs, and me plunging a needle into my arm." While it was true that the checks could ease her through emergencies, she came to realize that they were dangerous for her financial and emotional health.

15. Pay your bills on time. Record payment due dates on your calendar and mail your payments out, allowing extra days for them to be delivered and credited to your

account. The companies are not necessarily anxious for you to pay your bills on time because they profit from late charges, but being late can mar your credit report. One woman who used a Discover card simply to pay for the company's travel accident insurance—only $7.95 a month—was late with one payment. She was stunned to learn that this was recorded as a "30-day late" to the credit bureau and that her credit score was lowered a number of points.

16. Study your financial roots. Look back at your family history and consider the messages that were passed on to you about money. Perhaps there was a lot of drama and anger concerning money during your childhood. Could you be acting out what you learned? If so, figure out ways to break the family patterns. *What Mama Couldn't Tell Us About Love*, by Brenda Lane Richardson and Dr. Brenda Wade, is an excellent resource for breaking damaging family dynamics.

17. Invest money. Investments are like worker bees that keep going around the clock while you sleep and play. Talk to an investment counselor for help in making your money grow, and read Bridgforth's *Girl, Make Your Money Grow!* Her coauthor on this investment guide, Gail Perry Mason, whose story is included in the next chapter, helps clients choose stocks and other investments that reflect their values. Perry Mason can be contacted at gpmason2000@aol.com.

18. Generate extra cash. Consider your many God-given gifts and consider how you might use them to generate extra

cash. One of Glinda Bridgforth's clients used her strong organizational skills to help people organize their closets, garages, and offices. She used the extra money to pay off bills. Another used her cooking skills to sell homemade dinners to her fellow tenants. Other ideas for earning extra cash include: sewing and selling made-to-order quilts; restoring old furniture and selling the pieces; buying books from friends and associates and reselling them at a profit.

19. Enjoy your own reality show. It's easy to get caught up in the fantasy lives portrayed in television and film stories. Even when playing lowly paid workers, some stars inhabit the roomiest, most well-decorated apartments and wear the most fashionable clothing. On the other hand, characters driving older cars and wearing bargain clothing are portrayed as "losers." In truth, real losers are people who know better, but who waste their money anyway. Don't allow Hollywood images to ruin your relationship with the Almighty by constantly complaining to Him about what you don't have. By developing an attitude of gratitude you can learn to focus on the here and now. Thank God for gifts you might take for granted, including the vision that allows you to read these words and the chair you may be seated on, which offers physical support. As artist Henri Matisse once said, "There are flowers everywhere for those who bother to look."

20. Get thee to the library. Cancel your book club membership and visit your local library. If you don't see

books by your favorite authors, ask your librarian to do an interlibrary loan or order them. A free public library system is a blessing offered by few other countries. You may also want to buy more used paperbacks to cut back on spending. (Many used books are available at Amazon.com.) Another option is to start a book club at your church and offer to share or swap books with other avid readers.

PART VI

BLESSED

ENCOURAGEMENT

CHAPTER 16

Encouraging Others

I don't know about you, but when I see a film, I don't want to leave the theater dragging my feet and feeling hopeless. I like stories that leave me feeling hopeful. My favorite books are also the ones that leave me feeling hopeful. That's why I love reading scripture, and it's one more reason that I love the Lord. He is the bearer of good news about the Kingdom, offering us hope in salvation. In fact, the word "gospel" means good news. He encourages us through a method called "reframing."

That word means pretty much what it soun like. Imagine a picture of something that's so dreary, every time you glance at it, your spirits plummet. But take the picture off the wall, pull away the worn, dusty border, encase it in a beautiful frame, and suddenly you see the picture quite differently as you notice details that you missed earlier: The gilt frame shines and makes the colors appear more vivid. And now you can see that the objects in the picture symbolize treasures that seem within reach.

Jesus was a masterful teacher who used reframing to convey His message. In reminding us not to get caught up in day-to-day worries, he suggested that we see with new eyes, everyday, ordinary aspects of nature: "Look at the birds of the air; they neither sow nor reap nor gather into barns, and yet your heavenly Father feeds them. Are you of not more value than they?" (Matthew 6:26), and, He added: "Consider the lilies of the field, how they grow; they neither toil nor spin, yet I tell you, even Solomon in all his glory was not clothed like one of these" (Matthew 6:28–29).

The human mind is too complex, of course, to simply dismiss worries with a false sense of closure, and so God blessed us with the ability to encourage ourselves. During worrisome times it helps to find a quiet spot and sit comfortably, close your eyes, and breathe deeply. Even in a city as big and as busy as New York, I often find quiet spots. One of my favorites is a park behind the mayor's mansion, where I often sit beside the water to watch the waves dance and remind me how to get back into my flow and natural rhythm of life. Rather than trying to push your worries away, line them up like toy soldiers and let them pass through your consciousness. With God's help you are in control of those worries, and that means they can't crowd into your head and create a sense of panic, not if you remember the words of our Savior. Picture the birds and the lilies. Notice the details. See the birds swooping and playing and feeding their young. Remember that God provides. Watch as the lilies sway in the breeze, hundreds upon hundreds of them, representing God's abundance. After each vision, as you continue to breathe deeply and evenly, allow another concern to enter, followed by the bird and flower images. As you continue this meditation, your concerns subside, especially as you thank God for your many gifts, and ask Him to help you see your concerns in a new light. He will show you a way. Like the birds, your concerns will take flight. Like the lilies, your problems will be buried beneath the soil.

I hope this exercise allows you to tackle your problems with renewed courage. "Encouragement" means to arm with courage. God works through us to help us encourage one another, and I thank God for any opportunities He gives me to imitate and make visible signs of His Kingdom. It is the spirit of encouragement and hope that binds the Church together as we practice the ways of Jesus, who modeled the peaceable Kingdom.

As we continue exploring "blessed," through the final *E*, for encouragement, I urge you to look closely at the people whom you turn to for advice, and ask yourself whether they reflect the kind of encouragement all of us need. People are sometimes surprised to learn that four of my closest friends are seventy or older. I've always been drawn to older people, but perhaps especially since my mother's death, because I appreciate their wisdom and life experience. And I'm not talking dropping by to pay my respects a few times a year. No, these vibrant, brilliant, and wise folks could be considered my girlfriends. Well, that's not completely true, since one of them is male.

You may recall me mentioning earlier my spiritual advisor, the Reverend Doctor Elliott James Mason, Sr., who is eighty-three. He is such a gift in my life that sometimes, after a hard day, I return home and check my telephone messages, only to discover that he has called and left a prayer for me, my family, and my ministry. I often turn to him for advice and feel so blessed to even know this pious, God-fearing man.

My prayer partner—we meet at designated times throughout the week to pray for each other's concerns—is Mercedes Nesfield, who, at seventy-three, is a ball of energy. In 2002, I convinced her to start working with a personal exercise trainer, so she now does weight training, in addition to tennis and power walking.

Shortly after my mother's funeral, I grew much closer to Dr. Thelma C. Davidson Adair, eighty-five, a longtime and dear friend of my mother's. She and Mom, both of whom worked in the field of education and were natives of North Carolina, met in the 1940s, as two of a handful of African Americans in the predominantly white Presbyterian Church. And just as my mother had dedicated her life to encouraging others, so too had Dr. Adair.

Some people refer to her as the "Mother of Harlem." She and her husband, the Reverend Arthur Eugene Davidson, organized the Mount Morris Ascension Presbyterian Church, and she helped establish Mount Morris New Life, which operates a children's day-care center that today serves more than two hundred Harlem families. When the federal Head Start program began in 1965, Dr. Adair organized the programs now offered at five Harlem locations.

And just as Oprah has asked Maya Angelou to serve as village mother, because she appreciates her sage advice, I and several other women look to Dr. Adelaide L. Sanford, the New York State vice chancellor for the Board of Regents, the state's educational governing body. As the unofficial leader of our group, Isis, she is one of the most astounding speakers of our time. Because of her encouraging nature, she knows just how to get us talking, but she has a story of her own that needs to be told.

Decades ago, in the Bedford Stuyvesant area of Brooklyn, as the principal of P.S. 21, she helped build this failing public elementary school into one of the city's most high achieving. Her methods included teaching the parents and their children—most who lived in a nearby public housing project—about the glory of their African and African American ancestors. Dr. Sanford says, "We took down illustrations of our nation's leaders, such as those of George Washington and Benjamin Franklin from the walls, and replaced them with pictures of black people of achievement, who looked like the students." Plants and vases of flowers were set up in hallways, and in addition to instituting a more rigorous academic curriculum, she insisted that the children study black history and literature. "And I taught the parents that although they might not have much education, they had an inherited genius and they knew how to raise gifted children."

Twenty years after leaving her principal's post, Dr. Sanford is still stopped and thanked for her work, by graduates of P.S. 21, many of whom have gone into banking, education, and numerous other professional fields. The student she may have most impacted never attended her school, however. She met him a few years ago, after making a speech. "A tall, solidly built young man asked if he could speak to me, and when we were alone, he said, 'You saved my life.' I asked, 'Do I know you?' And he said I didn't know him, but that he knew me." He went on to say that several years earlier, he was a prisoner in solitary confinement. He said, 'I didn't care whether I lived or died, and didn't love anyone, including myself.' " Someone had given him a tape recorder and a tape of one of Dr. Sanford's speeches in which she spoke about the history of the African people, and she encouraged their descendants to honor those achievements by making the best of their lives. Hearing the tape changed him, he said. While still in prison, he worked hard to get his general equivalency diploma, and after his release attended college. He concluded with the news, "Now I'm getting a master's degree from Temple University."

A little bit of encouragement can go a long way. It's not something we do as Christians to be nice, it's what Christians are expected to do. On that note, I'd like to share the stories of two young women whose lives were saved by God through encouraging adults. Both are equally impressive human beings.

Gail Perry Mason, first vice president of investments for Oppenheimer, in Grosse Point, Michigan, is a wife as well as a mother of three sons. Most Tuesday evenings, she works with children at an orphanage, teaching them that it's practically sinful to not use the gifts God has given them. "When I first started working with these children, I asked them each to name the gifts that God had given them, and for them to tell me the ways in which they'd been blessed. They remained silent."

One older boy, attempting to speak for the other children, acknowledged that they all had gifts, but he said he didn't believe that they came from God. He demanded of Perry Mason, "If there's a God, why would he allow us to be here? If there's a God, why did some of us come from homes where our parents beat us or burned us or cut us?" When Perry Mason pointed out that there are lots of good people, the boy revealed a deep level of cynicism. He said, "Sure, there are corporations that contribute to places like this, but they only doing it for the tax write-offs. So where's the God that makes them good?" She was stunned by his words. "I wanted to answer him, but I was crying and didn't know what to say."

The next week, when Perry Mason returned, she asked the children to tell her what they wanted to be when they grew up. They

had big dreams, and she enjoyed listening to them. After they'd finished, she challenged the children, asking, "If God forgot about you,
where did you get the ability to sing ... and you, the ability to
draw ..." and she went around the room, having memorized their
dreams and respective talents. The children remained subdued, even
the boy who'd spoken for the others.

One little girl concluded, "I guess He didn't forget us, Ms. Mason." From there, her classes began. Through the years she has
helped these young people identify their talents and plan on using
them. If one wants to be a mechanic, for instance, Perry Mason re-
searches a range of salaries for mechanics, and then helps the individual see what that salary would afford. "We break it down. If they
want a certain car, then the child has to figure out how much that
will cost a month. If he wants to live in a certain place, we look at
the rents." Once expenses are added up, the child begins to grow
more realistic, perhaps deciding that an inexpensive Saturn might be
a safer bet than a sports car, until money is saved and invested.
Through the years she has worked with hundreds of children.

Her interest in the orphanage is personal. A few months after her
birth, Perry Mason, now forty-two, was given up for adoption—in
this place where she volunteers—by her white biological mother,
whose relatives were furious that she'd become pregnant by a black
man. There's a good chance that Perry Mason might have spent her
entire childhood in this place. She certainly wasn't considered most
likely to be adopted.

"I had hip dysplasia; my hip was deteriorating, and I couldn't
walk. I also couldn't talk by the age of three, and I was bald-
headed." Perry Mason thinks she was withering away, from lack of
love. "The staff was stretched thin and there was little time for each

child. I was picked up and played with for fifteen minutes a day, according to a schedule that was listed on a chart over my crib."

Despite a less than promising start, Perry Mason was adopted by a woman with meager financial resources, whose love and encouragement worked wonders. By the age of five, Perry Mason was not only walking, but running, and talking—in fact, her ability to speak is one of her gifts, along with a head for numbers and knack for making money for her clients.

By working with young people, Perry Mason hopes to return the investment her adopted mother made in her, and she works hard at it. She hasn't had a vacation in seventeen years, in part because she sponsors a summer camp for sixty African American children, many of them from extremely difficult circumstances. She pays for the endeavor out of her own pocket, and it costs her thousands of dollars, as she hires teachers who instruct them on everything from table manners to investing, and buys the children eyeglasses and pays for dental work—whatever is needed to help them return to school ready to learn.

Mason launches the first session of the summer camp by holding up a hundred dollar bill and asking if anyone wants it. This quickly gets the attention of the participants. Then she invites them to come up and stomp all over the bill. Once the frenzy ends, and Ben Franklin's face is scuffed and the bill frayed around the edges, Perry Mason asks if there's anyone out there who'd still like to have it. As the kids yell and shout and wave their hands, vying for the bill, she makes her message known: "Even though this bill has been through some hard times, it hasn't lost its value. Some of you in this room have been through hard times too, but you're still worthy. Your gifts are intact. Don't let anything stop you from performing at your highest level."

Perry Mason is inspirational, but so is Toni Daniels, whose story begins in Meridian, Mississippi, during the Jim Crow era, a time marked by the rigid enforcement of segregation. The early fifties were also a time when the dreaded polio epidemic killed and paralyzed thousands of Americans, many of them infants and children. By 1956, the disease was on the wane. A polio vaccine, introduced the year before, exposed children to a small dose of the virus that was designed to trigger their immune systems to produce chemicals that resisted the disease. In some cases, however, the inoculation actually gave people the disease. That's what may have happened to Toni Daniels, who at the time was a healthy three-year-old, living with her grandmother in Meridian while her parents worked to put money aside, hoping to give her and her brother a comfortable life.

Twenty-four hours after Toni's inoculation, the usually active child was bedridden, and her grandmother phoned the local physician and reported that the child was suffering with a sore throat, fever, and headache, early symptoms of the disease. "There were no black doctors practicing in the area," Toni recalls. Some white physicians treated their black patients scornfully, and the man her grandmother contacted was no different. "He dismissed her concerns, and insisted that I'd only come down with a cold." A few hours later, when her grandmother called again, reporting that Toni was showing signs of muscle weakness, another symptom of polio, the doctor told her not to call again.

"About two hours later, when she tried to wake me up, I was like a rag doll. I couldn't lift my head or sit up. She called my uncle, my mother's brother."

The two adults rushed her to the closest hospital, despite its policy of not treating black people. According to Daniels, "This white nurse took one look at me, and said, 'We don't know what she has, but we're not taking her.' "

Knowing that the polio virus spreads through the body like poison, attacking nerve cells and eventually an individual's nervous system, Daniels's grandmother and uncle drove fifty miles, to another hospital. The head nurse was just turning them away when proof was offered that God's spirit can overcome the most hateful circumstances. A white doctor intervened, telling the nurse, "You can't send her away. This child is in respiratory failure."

He was new at the job and young, but when the nurse warned him that he might get fired for treating Toni, he followed the example of Jesus, traveling through Galilee: "healing all manner of sickness and disease among the people" (Matthew 4:23).

Polio is not curable, and it had already marked little Toni's body. She was placed in an iron lung that helped her breathe, and once she was out, she wore a full body-brace until she was six years old. Today, however, thanks to ten surgeries and physical therapy, she can stand and walk and uses a scooter for traveling through hallways and streets.

Toni's grandmother reframed the story of what had happened in that emergency room, shaping the type of person she would become. "She didn't want to teach me to hate white people, and she didn't believe in hanging on to bitterness." Instead, they shared the good news. "They told me about a doctor risking his job to do what he knew was right, and how I'd been blessed."

This sense of being saved through God's grace later helped Daniels survive at the University of California, Los Angeles. While many of the school's 25,000 students have received exceptional levels of academic preparation, Daniels attended a school for handicapped children, which had not provided a challenging education. "I read only one book all the way through high school," Daniels says.

The university's admissions committee, realizing her great intelligence, did accept her, however. And she chose one of the most challenging majors: science, with classes that included calculus—which she failed. "I must have cried every day of my freshman year," she recalls. Help arrived in the form of another young black woman, Kathy Brown, who has since become a physician. "She'd noticed that I was often in the library, working really hard, and she asked me if I needed help." In the days and weeks to come, Kathy Brown would tutor Daniels and share her notes. If she didn't know a subject, she'd find someone who did. "Several of the other black students rallied around and helped me out." Through the years, Dr. Brown and Daniels have maintained a close friendship.

Daniels did graduate from UCLA, and later, in 1996, she earned a master's in business administration from Baruch College in New York, and she has since read enough books to make up for the lost years of reading. Her close involvement in the church has continued and led to her accepting a job as the executive director of enrollment at the General Theological Seminary in Manhattan, a postgraduate institution. Daniels is single, financially secure, and fit and independent. In fact, she's considering taking up the sport of hand-powered bicycling.

During the summer of 2005, Daniels attended the Billy Graham Crusade, along with hundreds of thousands of others. Reverend

Graham prayed for every facet of God's community to be transformed as the Gospel is proclaimed. Daniels looked around through the crowd and saw faces of every human shade—some heads were bowed, others lifted skyward, hands clasped, arms raised in joy—and she knew that she was alive and had been blessed with the ability to encourage others because the light of God is so mighty, it shines through the darkest of nights. To that I say, amen and hallelujah. Glory be to God, the highest.

PART VII

B
L
E
S
S
E
DEVOTION

CHAPTER 17

Devotion During Hard Times

As you turn to this last chapter and explore *D*, for devoted, in "blessed," you may wonder about the process that was used for selecting people with this final characteristic. The individuals whose stories appear in the preceding chapters have exemplified *Balance, Love, Energy, Spirit, Success,* and *Encouragement.* But this last characteristic, devotion to God, requires steadfast love and loyalty to God.

So how could I find people of such faith? The truth is you've already met them through their stories in this book. In some cases, there were stories of neglect, suffering, loss, and abuse, and yet these people kept loving God back, praising His name.

As testimony to the power of the Lord's message, those people were only a few among many. In fact, when planning this book, there was never even a need to draw up a list of those whose stories *had* to be included. Suddenly a name would happen to come up in a conversation or a usually difficult-to-reach individual would call out of the blue or suddenly become available at just the right moment. I

221

can only surmise that God's grace was involved in the process. And I thank Him for His devotion to us.

I have to admit that I was sometimes puzzled about the composite picture of those who generously shared their stories. For instance, I happen to know many people who live blessed lives, and that includes many singles. It turned out, however, that most of the individuals that were interviewed are happily married. I mention this to caution you against misinterpreting this as a sign that living a blessed life requires marriage. Instead, I view these numbers as a direct challenge to the widely held notion that there are no good men out there. You've probably heard this before, for it's a claim that's often made loudly and unabashedly.

In fact, when Brenda Lane Richardson was ready to mail off the manuscript for *What Mama Couldn't Tell Us About Love*—which includes suggestions for attracting "good" men—a postal clerk who'd asked about the subject of her work insisted that anyone who bought that book would be wasting money, because there are no good men. "They're all dogs," she added.

An elderly woman, who'd listened to the postal worker's tirade, said what everyone else within hearing distance seemed to be thinking. She told the young woman, "If that's what you believe, dear, is it any wonder you haven't found someone to love?"

I didn't share that story about how an individual's beliefs can shape her reality to suggest that all single people need attitude adjustments. But the old saying that "chance favors the well prepared" does often hold true. If the unexpected happens, we want to be at our very best. And God does offer us opportunities to grow and transform through even the most horrific experiences. Through discernment we move toward particular goals as Christians, so there's a good chance we'll encounter others who are seeking similar paths. If we don't get what we'd hoped and prayed for, however, it's certainly not because God favors one person more than another.

None of that seems to stop many of us from trying to explain God's intentions, but that is scarcely surprising. We live in a society in which answers are easy to come by, and this is, after all, the Information Age. Want to know how to take the salt out of a ham? We can get online and get an answer. Want to know how to take off ten pounds of unwanted weight? There are shelves full of "proven" weight-loss methods at the local Barnes and Noble. And thanks to an explosion in scientific knowledge, researchers know more about the human body and the mysteries of the universe than ever before. With so many answers a short reach away, it's no wonder that we try to devise easy answers even to the toughest questions, including those that are related to God.

The question regarding why some of us have love in our lives and why others do not seems almost easy in the face of what I call the Big One. Think back on some of those stories you've read, and you may wonder why God would allow such terrible things to occur. It's the most sensitive question of all, perhaps especially because the "wrong" answer can easily offend people of faith. But I believe devotion to God requires us to explore difficult questions, rather than accepting pat and easy answers. This helps us to serve Him better and deepens our faith. For that reason, I'd like to explore some popular fallacies of why bad things happen to good people.

I. We're all born sinners and have to suffer the consequences.
   The notion of original sin is that Adam and Eve's failures
   in the Garden of Eden damaged human nature, and as

such we are all innately predisposed to be sinful and can't overcome this without God's intervention. Simply put, Adam's fall sent human beings into eternal damnation. Well, I do think we're all innately sinful, in our thoughts if not our behaviors, and that as human beings we can't possibly live up to God's perfection. But I take comfort in the image of God as the forgiving Father who welcomes us home. It is only by an act of grace on the cross that we are saved. And I thank and praise Him for giving His only begotten Son, Jesus Christ, Our Lord, who died for our sins. So it doesn't make sense that God would continue to punish us through eternity for our inborn imperfections.

2. God punishes us for our individual sins, and a child's suffering is payment for the sins of the parents. I've often visited parishioners in the wake of tragedies and heard them blame themselves. Someone will say that the sudden death of a child, for instance, is God's way of punishing parents for not keeping up tithe payments or having an abortion long ago. Their need to blame, to put the onus on someone is understandable, but I hasten to assure them that God would never punish them in this manner.

In fact, this subject is discussed in John 9:3, when Jesus is questioned about whether a man who is blind from birth is suffering from his own sins or those of his parents. The Lord refutes the notion that human tragedy is God's punishment for sin. I have no reason to doubt the Lord, and would never believe that our Heavenly Father would ever make innocent children pay the price for their parents' sins.

The idea that if we're evil we'll be punished by God,

and if we're good we'll be blessed by Him is an example of cause-and-effect theory. And there is scripture to support it. "Tell the innocent how fortunate they are, for they shall eat the fruit of their labors. Woe to the guilty! How unfortunate they are, for what their hands have done shall be done to them" (Isaiah 3:10–11). And, according to a proverb, "No harm befalls to the righteous, but the wicked have their fill of trouble" (Proverbs 12:21). Agnostics contrast passages such as these with Jesus's condemnation of the idea that human tragedy is punishment for sin and describe them as contradictory statements. They seem to have missed the point that these would only be contradictory if they had been written by one person. As we know, one of the reasons the Bible is so powerful is that it was recorded by various people who were faithful to their understanding of God.

The cause-and-effect theory of why people suffer is not easily sustained because, as we've often seen, evil doesn't discriminate between good and bad. Time and time again, we see instances in which good people, including innocent children, suffer. For that matter, a lot of evil people suffer too. In the Sermon on the Mount, Jesus points out that God causes the sun "to rise on the evil and on the good, and sends rain on the righteous and on the unrighteous" (Matthew 5:45). One indication of this truth is that some people, who boast of having turned their backs on God, enjoy comfortable lives that include everything from good health to loving families to financial prosperity. I pity these people. They lack a close relationship with the Almighty. But this is a choice the individual has made.

3. God gives us pain so we can become better people. Paul does say that we are made worthy for the kingdom of God through suffering. "We suffer with Him, that we may be also glorified together" (Romans 8:17). And we are told, "through many tribulations we must enter the kingdom of God" (Acts 14:22). This does not mean that God causes us to suffer, but that we have the chance to become closer to Him in our suffering. One example of this is the suffering that slaves endured in the United States. For more than two hundred years, African Americans were beaten and reviled, the women raped, and families sold away. Their response to this suffering was to turn to God in song and words of praise. Millions came away from the experience with so many gifts, such as faith, creativity, and sense of humor. Their faith sustained them and brought out their absolute best.

Given my beliefs about human tragedies, I cannot blame God for our grief and misery. These seem to be more likely explanations for why humankind suffers.

• Free processes in the world. In nature, one act sets off another. For instance, lightning might strike and cause a forest fire, which wipes out thousands of trees. God doesn't stage-manage every natural event, and the same goes for His involvement in our behavior. We too have been given the power to act freely, and those who choose to do evil may negatively affect others. As a result we all absorb the weight of other people's choices. If someone drinks and drives, he or she might strike a child with a car and kill him. God's not causing the suffering of the child or those who love him—it is the act of an individual.

• Effects of nature. Genetics may be the cause of death or suffering. A genetic mutation, such as a bad heart, may be passed on from a parent to child. Also, environmental conditions, like a polluted stream, might cause disease, suffering, and death. And random events such as an accident might occur. In one instance, during an informal school meeting, a young man was sitting on a classroom window ledge. Another student asked to sit beside him, and he reached down and extended a hand to help lift her up. His hand slipped out of hers, and he fell backward out of the window. He died from the impact of hitting the pavement. No alcohol or drugs were found in his system. No one and nothing was to blame for his death. It was purely a random accident.

You may disagree with me about why we suffer. I certainly don't claim to have all the answers. It might be helpful, though, to remember that when Job was crying out about his losses, God challenged him in the same way he challenges us, asking, "Where were you when I laid the foundation of the earth?" (Job 38:4). He was reminding us that we will never understand all of His mysteries. What He wants us to do is to love and trust him despite our lack of understanding. This is true devotion. In the end, it doesn't really matter why He allows us to suffer. What counts is our response to the pain. We must forever continue to praise and thank Him for being the welcoming Father, the confident Father, who runs alongside us, promising that He will be there whenever we need Him. Breaking away from that loving Father is a terrible loss indeed.

We end on a high note, for we are filled with the hope of all that awaits those of us who remain devoted, those of us who take His advice. The answer can be found in a psalm that happened to be a favorite of my parents. Throughout my childhood, I heard them repeat it so many times, that I can still hear their voices as they repeat it together. I invite you to say it along with me, picturing all that we can expect from the Lord when we remain in relationship with Him and enjoy the blessed life.

The 23rd Psalm

The Lord is my Shepherd; I shall not want.

He maketh me to lie down in green pastures:

He leadeth me beside the still waters.

He restoreth my soul:

He leadeth me in the paths of righteousness for His name's sake.

Yea, though I walk through the valley of the shadow of death,

I will fear no evil:

For thou art with me;

Thy rod and thy staff, they comfort me.

Thou preparest a table before me in the presence of mine enemies;

Thou annointest my head with oil;

My cup runneth over.

Surely goodness and mercy shall follow me all the days of my life,

and I will dwell in the House of the Lord forever.